EMBEDDED ENEMY

The Insider Threat

Donna

BART E. WOMACK

Thank you for the opportunity to be a guest on your show. Enjoy the read.

Best Bart

INSPIRE ON PURPOSE
Changing Lives With Words

EMBEDDED ENEMY: The Insider Threat

Copyright © 2013 by Bart E. Womack

Inspire On Purpose Publishing
909 Lake Carolyn Parkway, Suite 300
Irving, Texas 75039
(888) 403-2727

http://inspireonpurpose.com

The Platform Publisher™

Printed in the United States of America

Library of Congress Control Number: 2013948201

ISBN 10: 0989800806

ISBN 13: 978-0-9898008-0-8

* Disclaimer: The names of the soldiers, families, and some military personnel described in this book may have been changed for reasons of privacy. The details contained herein are based on the best recollection of those who contributed information in an attempt to piece together the timeline and chain of events on that fateful day.

For media inquiries or general information, please:
Call: 1.800.349.5113
Email Promotional Team: speaker@promoteonpurpose.com
Email Bart Directly: bart@embeddedenemy.com

With the utmost sincerity, I'd like to thank the members of our Bastogne Brigade Headquarters team for their many contributions to this project. Without your input, support and blessing to proceed, it would not have been possible to tell our story. It was an honor to serve beside you and I'm proud to have you as friends.

*   *   *   *   *

Together, we dedicate this book to our comrades who lost their lives to terrorism:

Captain Christopher Seifert ~ United States Army
and
Major Gregory Stone ~ United States Air Force

*   *   *   *   *

From the moment of this book's inception, I knew something good had to come from that night. Therefore, a portion of the proceeds are donated to the Benjamin Seifert Scholarship Fund.

CONTENTS

SECTION 1
UNSUSPECTING COMRADES

CHAPTER 1
5-Minute Mayhem

The 101st Airborne Division soldiers in Bastogne Brigade of Fort Campbell, KY, were sitting in Kuwait, just outside of Iraq in a sandcastle dubbed Camp Pennsylvania. We were waiting for the order to cross the border into Iraq and take down our sworn enemy.

We had prepared for this moment for 812 days—that is every moment of every day since the cowardly attacks of September 11, 2001.

Some of us had been together for years while others met us the day we landed in the sand. But we all had been trained by the best military organization in the world. No matter how long we had been together, we were a well-oiled machine, confident we could take on the world.

For the past 18 months, my group—the Bastogne Brigade—had many stops and starts before getting to Kuwait. We had been pulled from our war mission to guard the gates of our home—Fort Campbell, KY—after the September 11 attacks on American soil.

We were later sent on side trips to the Joint Readiness Training Center in Fort Polk, LA, for training; to Jordan twice for a Joint Training Exercise with Omani soldiers; and on a support mission to train the cadets at the United States Military Academy at West Point, NY.

When we finally got the official orders to join the fight in Iraq, after all of the false rumors and added training and signing of wills and saying good-byes to loved ones—while reassuring them that we fully expected to return—and packing and putting bills on autopay, we were excited to finally be part of the war-fight.

Landing in Kuwait and arriving at Camp Pennsylvania was our ticket to the show.

This massive, four-square mile, octagonal dust bowl, found only by a GPS with proper coordinates, was exactly where we wanted to be. We had waited a long time to get here.

Camp Pennsylvania was built by pushing sand and dirt from the inside out to form earthen walls that were eight-feet tall and 10-feet wide. Just inside the walls, spaced every 300 meters, were guard towers about 15-feet tall, each manned with two soldiers around the clock. They were equipped with a set of binoculars that let the guards see for miles. Each tower had 24/7 communication ties to the Tactical Operation Center, or Command Center, and to the officer in charge.

The camp was made up of seven pads. The Brigade headquarters pad contained 10 small tents. The other pads had about 20 tents each. At headquarters, our tents housed the senior leadership of the commanding officer, an array of staff officers, and some senior noncommissioned officers.

Tents the size of those at a carnival or festival, which we called "Fest Tents," were the sleeping quarters for most of the soldiers. Each Fest Tent could comfortably hold about 75 soldiers. Those were primarily found on the other six pads.

Each of the seven pads had its own water source, seatless port-a-johns, and maintenance pads to do maintenance on the vehicles when they arrived.

The camp was also equipped with a wash rack to wash the vehicles, a container yard, a trash dump, an ammunition holding area, and a burn yard to burn classified material if necessary. More importantly, it had a separate area for morale, welfare, and recreation, with a small basketball court, a gym, a small area to watch satellite television, and separate rooms for reading and board games.

We also had telephones. If a soldier had an extra two hours of time to wait in a line to talk for a few minutes, we could find them here. Once they made it to the front of the line, they had to shell out about $2 a minute after a connection charge.

The high cost of saying "I love you" in the desert didn't stop us from calling.

Once that one guy in a company called home to his wife, she undoubtedly told the other spouses in the company, which meant that all of the spouses and significant others would sit at home waiting for the phone to ring. The pressure to call would mount in the company, and more and more the soldiers found themselves back in those long lines to make that call, but this time it was to stay out of trouble.

The ground was hard packed with a light dusting of sand that flowed freely from the slightest of breezes. This would be our temporary home until we were called up for the fight.

The Screaming Eagles of the Bastogne Brigade were chomping at the bit to partner with our fellow soldiers in the fight against Saddam Hussein and his weapons of mass destruction. We were ready to find Osama bin Laden in whatever cave he was bunkered. We wanted to serve our country, to defend America against its enemies.

We were ready for anything.

As the days passed and we arrived at day number 22, still sitting on the border of Kuwait and Iraq had us all on edge. We knew at any minute the fight could start since we were so close to the action, but it also seemed unlikely to happen for some time. It was another "hurry up and wait" order from higher up. We knew the drill. We hated the drill. But we knew it to be a part of the job for which we signed on.

As we waited, all 4,000 of us newcomers scrambled to try to get one of the 500 cots left behind by the previous brigade that had already been sent forward. The brigade that had been sent on took the rest of the cots and the port-a-john toilet seats as a heady welcome to us, the newest warfighters. They were kind enough to leave one TV with limited satellite service, a handful of Internet connections for our computers, and of course, the two-hour wait on the phone to call home.

Although the calls home were expected and appreciated, they contained little substance since the list of things we could not say overshadowed the things we could.

I didn't really have anyone to call. My newly remarried ex-wife would not be expecting my call, even if it did only pertain to our boys. I was confident that she would take good care of them. The first good-bye had been hard enough on both my 11- and seven-year-old boys. I was afraid a call would only make things worse for them.

The only thing waiting for me back home was our brigade mascot, Bastogne. I missed the slobbering American bulldog pup with the occasional gastrointestinal slips, and was far less confident that the rear detachment soldiers were taking good care of him.

So the Bastogne Brigade waited.

Idling in this holding pattern, I slept in the same tent as the Commander. This meant that I had only two roommates and a lot of legroom. I was able to fit in a ragtag wall locker that a fellow non-commissioned officer found for me. It was just sitting out by itself in the middle of Camp Pennsylvania's desert landscape, calling my name.

It was no secret among my fellow soldiers that I was a little obsessive-compulsive. I was a neat freak long before I joined the Army, and the Army rewarded my behavior. So when my long-time comrade saw the unclaimed locker, he knew I would appreciate it the most. I was very excited to have a place to properly store my meager Army possessions.

My desert roommates—Brigade Commander Colonel Frederick Benjamin Hodges and Brigade Executive Officer Major Kenneth Romaine—were some of the best leaders the Army had to offer. Romaine was a graduate of the School of Advanced Military studies, known by insiders as the "Military Jedi Knights." They were a specially selected group of leaders who possessed the flexibility of mind to solve complex operational and strategic problems in peace, conflict, and war. His skills would soon be tested.

Commander Hodges had known back in Kentucky that we would all be tested on the battlefield soon enough. Immediately upon his arrival, Hodges started to make the Bastogne Brigade a solid team. He introduced us all to "Ultimate Football," and the concept of "Mangudai" to the officers.

Ultimate Football has minimal rules. It was named after Ultimate Frisbee, but that's about where the similarities end. I was lucky to be on Hodges' team the first day we played. We won. That was almost a guarantee since only Hodges knew the rules.

Eventually, everyone in the Bastogne Brigade learned the so-called rules. We actually learned that more rules were added in the middle of the game, often during play, even while the ball was in the air. Basically, if you could catch and throw, you could play. To play successfully, you had to be comfortable being constantly on the move and playing offense and defense, all within seconds of each other. We even played with two footballs at once.

This very simple game brought out the competitiveness to fight until the end, and not to settle for defeat. It also brought us together as a team within the headquarters and the Brigade Combat Team. (Our Brigade was smaller, consisting of three battalions, and the Brigade Combat Team (BCT) was larger, consisting of seven; we all worked together.) Ultimate Football with its entrenched team-building efficacy had become a trademark in the Bastogne Brigade Combat Team.

We quickly learned that the art of team building was a forte for Hodges—and he wasn't done. He theorized about a training exercise and team-building event that he had seen years ago. The theory quickly moved into the planning stages, and it came with yet another one of Hodges' exclusive names . . . "Mangudai."

The Mangudai were a military unit of the Mongols, their version of our special forces. The training exercise sent the leaders on long, physically demanding missions. These elite warriors, dating back to the 13th century, were put through an arduous gauntlet, comprised of minimal food and sleep, extreme conditions, and strenuous scenarios to prove themselves worthy of the toughest missions.

The first phase of our version of Mangudai started in Dahlonega, GA, at the U. S. Army's Mountain Ranger Camp. For two days and two nights, the officers would experience rapid changes of leadership positions as they made their way up and down the treacherous terrain.

To challenge their intestinal fortitude, famished leaders were given small bags of rice and sardines to eat. The leaders displayed incredulity when they received the same meager meal an actual Mongol warrior would have received. Although they were highly disgruntled, they ate the protein and carb-packed meal anyway, if only for energy.

Having passed the mind game and gut-check test, the officers were escorted to the mess hall for a goliath breakfast of bacon, eggs, pancakes, grits . . . the works.

Part two of the Mangudai adventure was a team-building event. The leaders were taken to Currahee Mountain where they would relive a scene inspired from the epic film Band of Brothers by running up Currahee Mountain, the same mountain the soldiers of the 101st Airborne Division had run up before jumping on D-Day in 1944.

Despite the pouring rain, the leaders ran up Currahee led by Colonel Hodges. At least for the next 40 minutes, they too felt like a "band of brothers."

Hodges loved these sorts of events because they focused on leader training and team building and gave the Soldiers stories to tell.

Inspired by the Band of Brothers connection, Hodges directed that the emblem of a club be sewn on the helmets of all the soldiers in the 327th Infantry Regiment, just like our Screaming Eagle forefathers had done. He asked that the units in the entire BCT do the same; they respectfully complied.

While Ultimate Football appeared to be just some chaotic fun and Mangudai merely a reenactment of ancient warriors, they would teach the Bastogne Brigade some very valuable lessons in teamwork, which included flexibility, accountability, and versatility. Even Hodges would be surprised at how valuable those lessons would be in the days to come.

* * *

We often referred to Iraq as the "land of not quite right." When deployed to developing nations, our collective experience found that local craftsmen could always get the job done, but the final result was rarely what we envisioned. So when I looked at the tangle of cable wire making our television function in my

Camp Pennsylvania tent, I thought, "Here I am again, in the 'land of not quite right.'"

Even though I questioned how it could even work, I knew that I had to accept it. It wasn't like I could call the local cable or satellite provider to come to fix it. Even though the locals seemed to make things work with Band-Aids and bubble gum, I knew that anyone else messing around with it would have destroyed the signal. Still, I worried that the whole thing was going to go up in flames in an electrical fire one day.

One benefit of waiting—and sleeping in the Commander's tent—was that I had access to the one television set in the whole camp. On it, I could watch my favorite sport, golf, and my favorite golfer, Tiger Woods. And as we waited on that 23rd day, I got to enjoy both.

The calendar had just barely turned to the 23rd day—0100 hours, or 1 a.m., on March 23, 2003, when it happened.

I should have been sleeping, but every swing Tiger made from the tee could be the last one I saw for a long time. We never knew exactly when we would be called up to cross into Iraq. So, I planned my whole day around the Bay Hill Invitational golf tournament starring Tiger Woods.

My golf hero was just teeing off on the 9th hole. He had won this tournament for the past three years, and I was hoping to see him once again lap the field. Leading by six strokes, he was well on his way to dominating the game and winning three majors, like he did in 2000.

As I settled in to watch, I heard the canvas of the tent's flap ruffle against the wooden floor. I looked up to see the Brigade Executive Officer, Major Kenneth Romaine, emerge from the dark, short vestibule that led into our tent. He was returning from the Tactical Operations Center, which is the Command Center for Camp Pennsylvania.

"How's everything?" I asked.

"Good," Romaine said. "They're doing good. I'm going to bed. Is Tiger still kicking butt?"

"Yep, six-shot lead with nine holes yet to play."

"Wow."

My eyes went back to the computer as Romaine walked behind me toward the end of the table and into his sleeping area.

As I concentrated on Tiger's swing and listened for the sweet THWACK of the ball, I heard the tent flap flutter again and a scraping sound as something rolled toward me. It was almost as if Tiger's ball had made it all the way into our own Kuwaiti sand trap.

However, the object that had just rolled into the tent was no golf ball.

The hand grenade rolled between Tiger and me, resting at the tent's edge. I was sitting at the far end of the table. Had I been sitting one inch to the left, or leaning forward, I may not have seen what actually rolled into the tent and landed only five feet away.

Sparks emitted from the hand grenade. I remember wondering why it was sparking instead of just blowing, and that it looked like those "not quite right" spaghetti wires from the cable television that could start a cheap version of Fourth of July fireworks.

It is amazing how quickly thoughts can ping through your mind. I knew grenades only took five seconds to blow, and I think I wasted two seconds coming to the shocking realization of what was happening.

I looked up and saw Romaine staring at me with his eyes open wide. We knew that we had to get out fast. I sprinted faster than Carl Lewis to clear what I thought was the blast area, and then tore to the rear of the tent to wake up Colonel Hodges, the only other person in the tent.

Colonel Hodges was a West Point graduate who took over as our Commander less than a year before the grenade rolled into our tent. He had whipped the Bastogne Brigade into shape with constant readiness drills back home in Fort Campbell. Until this second, none of us would really know how ready we were—or were not.

As I dashed to rouse Hodges, I passed Romaine as he pondered his next move. I had no idea this would be the last time I would see him until the smoke cleared.

Something about having your ass about to be blown off makes you move at the speed of light. I felt like I had just run a life-saving, 100-meter dash. It was the adrenaline rush of my first near-death experience. My throat was dry. I felt choked. I swallowed repeatedly to lubricate my tongue and throat so that I could talk. When I got to the Colonel, he was dead asleep.

"Sir, get up," I said frantically, as I shook him hard enough to rattle his dog tags. "There's a grenade about to go off up front."

Looking back, I now realize that the five seconds I had before a grenade blew was long over. At the time, all I knew was that the tent was filling with smoke. I wondered if maybe it was a "not quite right" homemade grenade, and that we had gotten lucky.

I later discovered that the grenade was an "incendiary grenade" which is designed to catch everything on fire, instead of exploding and spraying shrapnel. The grenade emits a flame like that of a blowtorch when the knob is first turned to ignite it. What we were experiencing was the fire and smoke from that first grenade of the attack—the first of what would ultimately be four grenades thrown into three tents.

The grenade had worked just fine, filling our tent with thick smoke and catching it on fire.

As the disoriented Colonel slipped on his boots, he hurriedly looked for his weapon to prepare for the attack. His pistol was in its shoulder holster, draped across his load-bearing vest he'd hung on the chair right beside his sleeping mat. Yet in the thick smoke, his weapon was invisible.

Eager to get out of harm's way, I clutched Hodges' left arm to steer him to stand upright. We had no time for him to tie boots and no time for me to enforce uniform standards. The warfight had started, and we had to fight it with what we had right then.

The Colonel wanted to move directly to the front to get out of the tent, not aware that the grenade's kill zone was in that direction. I grabbed him again by the arm.

"Wait, the grenade is that way and it's about to explode," I yelled, still unaware of how much time had passed.

Seconds were passing, and time felt as if it were speeding up. Each split second, a decision was being made to save our lives. By then our tent was so dark, black, and smoke filled, we couldn't even see the fluorescent lights that were on in our tent just a couple of minutes before that first grenade.

It was so dark, in fact, that we could have closed our eyes, put a black bag over our heads, and still had better vision than in the tent. Colonel Hodges was right beside me and I simply could not see him, so I moved on instinct.

Using Hodges' sleeping mat to align with the center aisle, I turned and yelled to Hodges as loud as I could, "Ready—Go!"

In the confusion, we did not hear the second grenade roll into the tent. This one was a fragmentary grenade, the kind that does explode.

We were in escape mode, not knowing what had just rolled under the flap. We both jetted off of the blocks like Olympic runners. I started out on the left, the same side of the tent as the first grenade, and Colonel Hodges was on the right.

I ran as fast as I could because I never really heard an explosion. I ran hunched over, with my left shoulder higher than my right, up around the height of my ear, to protect myself from the blast that I prayed had already happened.

The tent had only one opening and only one person could fit through the tent flap at a time. The adrenaline flowing added to my speed, so I had to slow down so that the Colonel could make it out of the exit before me.

My plan didn't work so well.

The second grenade—the fragmentary grenade—exploded just as we started to run out of the tent.

No more than two strides into our sprint, the explosion's concussive force knocked the Colonel down and backwards into his sleeping area. I had no idea what happened to him.

At 6'2" and 230 pounds, the Colonel was certain that a large person knocked him down. He didn't hear the explosion and was sure that the enemy was in the tent with him. He now frantically began searching for the pistol he had failed to locate a few minutes earlier.

On his hands and knees, he made his way back to the chair by his sleeping mat. Rummaging in the dark, he found his vest with his weapon hanging where he had left it. Once he pulled his standard-issue 9mm out of the holster and into his right hand, his firing hand, he could barely hold it. He immediately realized that his arm was injured.

His first thought was that he had a broken arm because he couldn't even secure the grip of the pistol. He was mad and let out his frustration, "I cannot believe that we deploy, and now I have a broken arm."

He had no idea of the extent of his injury.

At the same time that the Colonel was flying backwards from the blast, Major Romaine was feeling the full force of the second grenade. Unaware of the second grenade, Romaine moved deeper into the tent to get away from the first grenade that was still smoking.

Luckily for Romaine, the Brigade was preparing to move out in a couple of days and had packed duffle bags, cartons of water, and boxes of MREs, or Meals Ready to Eat. The packed supplies were stacked close to the wall locker I had snagged earlier to house my personal items. That second grenade rolled near our packed gear and the wall locker, allowing the gear to take the brunt of the blast.

Had all of our pre-packed supplies and my contraband wall locker not been placed exactly where they were—especially the locker—Romaine would have caught a much larger piece of the blast.

In fact, that second fragmentary grenade rolled just two feet from where I would have been sleeping if Tiger weren't playing golf. To this day, I credit both the wonderful game of golf and the superlative golfer, Tiger Woods, for saving my life. For this, I will always view him with the utmost esteem.

Disoriented from the concussion of the blast but still standing, Romaine realized that the blast was a grenade. A split second later, all of those lessons from a career of training came flooding back.

We learned that when grenades are tossed, a rifle squad usually follows right behind the explosion. Anywhere from two to nine soldiers could be following into the blast area to clear the space with small-arms fire. Romaine's adrenaline and automatic pilot sent him scrambling for his weapon.

He grabbed his pistol out of the holster. Romaine cocked and chambered a round. He waited a few seconds for that first guy to come through the vestibule and into the tent.

Nobody came in.

Armed and ready for the onslaught, Romaine sat prepared just outside the vestibule of our tent's only opening. With his pistol drawn and ready, Romaine expected to see armed enemies flowing inside to clear the tent.

He kept moving until he got to the vestibule where it was darker than it was in the tent. He paused, wondering where the lights were and trying to acclimate to the dark.

Every night before that night, the headquarters outside area had been well lit by a powerful generator. We all thought the grenade blew out the interior tent lights but could not figure out what happened to the outside lights. It would be much later before we discovered the outside lights were doused as part of a bigger plan by our attacker.

I continued down the aisle toward the area where the grenades had gone off and where Romaine absorbed the concussion of the blast. I had to trust the Colonel was a step in front of me because I could not even see my own hand in front of my face, so I had no way of verifying his location.

When I reached the darkest and most smoke filled part of the tent, my adrenaline was pumping through me, making it hard to hear anything more than my own heartbeat. Though I never heard the blast and visibility was zero, I kept moving.

It was so dark and smoky that I lost sight of the Colonel. I continued to run in that same direction toward the unzipped side. Somehow I was able to make it through—pure luck in the dark.

I cleared the flap that led into the vestibule. It was the only part of the tent that wasn't completely engulfed in smoke. I knew someone was there, and since I hadn't been shot, it must be a fellow American soldier. It was my Executive Officer, Major Romaine.

As I ran past Romaine, I heard boots scraping the wooden pallets. He was moving much more slowly than I was. I just knew the Colonel had to be outside already.

I felt the cold, crisp air hit my face as I burst into the night. In a matter of seconds, it rushed up through my nose and down my throat. I could breathe again. That first breath cleared my lungs of all the smoke that I had ingested in the tent.

Once the smoke cleared from my head and the cold desert air slapped across my face, I slowly took back control of my body from the adrenaline-fueled sprinting.

We had no idea what hit us.

CHAPTER 2
Teamwork

Those first five minutes of the assault felt like only 30 seconds. Though my heart was beating fast, pounding like a base drum, I had to be in control.

I quickly gained my bearings and made a 180-degree scan from my left to my right, expecting to find Colonel Hodges nearby. He should have been out of the tent well before me. He wasn't there.

As I stood gasping for air, I realized something was different. Something had changed. The generator light was not illuminating the headquarters area as it had for the past three weeks. I guessed that it was inoperable, likely running out of the diesel fuel that it needed to function. What a time to break down!

I had just run from dark to pitch dark. I knew that I could find my natural night vision, if I had the time to allow my eyes to adjust to the dark environment.

As my mind raced to make a plan, Romaine was crouching in our tent's vestibule, 30 feet behind me. He heard some movement and uttered something in that direction. He turned, but did not see any movement.

A second later, Romaine was shot.

* * *

The momentum from my run out of the burning tent had carried me onto the sandy gravel and well past the Texas barriers (named after the state of Texas because of their massive size) in front of our tent.

Totally confused, I could not understand why our tent was burning, grenades were exploding, and now shots were being fired at my comrades.

I spun around in the direction of the gunshot and slid into the rocks while reaching down with my right hand to unsnap my holster and draw my standard Army issue M9 Beretta with a custom grip that I had personally installed.

It had been my baby for just short of two years. This was the first time that I had drawn it with the intent of shooting another human being. I quickly charged it and aimed it in the direction of where I heard the shot fired at Romaine.

As I charged my 9mm with its quick-load magazine, I could feel that the round failed to chamber and that the bolt never moved forward. Suddenly there was a picture hovering above my head, like in a cartoon, vividly showing me my ammunition and unloaded magazines, sitting on the conference table. I was immediately reminded that I had no ammunition.

My rounds were left to burn with the television set and the rest of the items in the tent. Now I had the added concern that the rounds could possibly cook off if they got too hot, and within seconds, fire like mini projectiles coming from an unknown direction.

I had to focus now on how to immediately arm myself and to find, fix, and neutralize the person or persons who were throwing grenades and shooting at us. I turned away from the direction of our tent, holstering my now useless weapon and moving toward the Tactical Operations Center or TOC.

I hoped that I could quickly grab a weapon and some ammunition, find Major Romaine, locate Colonel Hodges, and be on the hunt for insurgents—all within minutes. I had no time to waste, so I had to rely on my instincts honed from years of military training.

With the lights out and thick smoke hanging in the air, I couldn't see a thing. My sprint to the Command Center was taken on faith, gravel spraying out from under my feet as I bolted in the direction of the TOC.

My plan was to secure a weapon, any weapon, preferably a fully automatic M4 assault rifle with a cyclic rate of fire of 700-950 rounds per minute. At a length of just over 29 inches, with the stock retracted, it is the weapon of choice for close-quarters combat, due to its compact size and firepower. I was hoping that I didn't need that many rounds, nor did I want to carry them. It was nice to know I had the capability—just in case.

The only thing I knew was that I needed something light so I could move fast, and something that would produce the most casualties.

If I had time for a wish list, I was hoping to also find a couple of magazines with extra rounds and a pair of Night Vision Devices, also known as NODs, to give me a better view of what we were up against. I knew I needed to "own the night" if I was to emerge in one piece on the other side of this attack.

* * *

The round that hit Romaine landed squarely in his shooting hand. The bullet had a life of its own as it sliced through his shooting hand, penetrated his other hand, and deflected right down through his left leg.

The damaging ricochet did not feel lucky to Romaine, but it turned out to be the best of the worst things that could happen to him. Romaine didn't have time to find his vest in the dark, so his core was exposed in the smoke-filled tent. By pointing his pistol out in front of him and preparing to shoot, only his exposed hands were shot. If his hands hadn't been out in front of him, he would have likely been shot in the upper torso or chest.

Romaine took a step back into the tent's vestibule—not that it was going to provide true cover—but so that he wouldn't be in plain view. He knelt in place, expecting the enemy to come around the corner, shoot him again, and then try to enter the tent.

Looking down at his weapon, Romaine tried to operate his Beretta 9mm now covered with dark, thick, gooey blood from his hands. Unfortunately, it was too slick to hold. He looked at his hands and both of them were ripped open and profusely bleeding.

He knew that he still had to defend himself when the enemy came around the corner and into the vestibule. His only protection was to surprise the enemy first, by jumping him or tackling him.

Twenty seconds . . . and then 30 seconds went by . . .

Romaine began to feel a warm trickle go down his leg. He reached down to feel the trickle, moving his hand all over that area and slid his finger into a hole that the bullet had made in his leg.

He was reminded of the stories about guys getting hit in an artery and bleeding out. If it happened, it happened, but he wasn't going to sit there and let it happen all because he was waiting on someone to come around the corner. He thought that the only way to survive was to keep moving.

* * *

As I formulated my plan to grab the necessary equipment and return to help my comrades, a second fragmentary grenade, the third grenade of the night, rocked the Kuwaiti desert.

I didn't hear that one go off either.

All I knew for sure was that I wasn't hit, I was able to move, and I hadn't broken my stride. I never stopped to ask myself, "What if this was a coordinated attack?"

A coordinated attack is a planned and synchronized attack that employs various elements of a command to use its force to its greatest advantage. If the enemy had enough intelligence on us to know that our tent was where the Commander, Executive Officer, and the Command Sergeant Major were, then they probably would know where our Command Center, or TOC, was.

That meant the TOC had to be next on the hit list. I prayed that it had not yet been hit and occupied by the enemy. If it was already occupied, I could have very well been running into an ambush.

I ran through the dark and flung open the flap of the TOC tent entrance—the interior light was low, as if someone had dimmed it on purpose. I was relieved that I could finally see something and that an ambush was not waiting for me.

Now walking at a fast pace, I breezed through the front portion of the TOC, passing by two soldiers from the National Guard unit that were part of what we called "the Mayor's Cell." The Mayor's Cell was in charge of all of the logistics that made the camp function—water, food, facilities, etc. That freed our leadership to just plan and prep for the War.

The Guardsmen were as confused as I was about what exactly was going on. However, their training had taken hold, and they were prepared. As the Guardsmen stood off to the side and out of my way, the disconcerting looks on their faces told me they were nervously watching for the enemy.

Had I been in their position—inside a tent with explosions and gunfire happening on the outside—I would have been guarding the door. So as their superior Noncommissioned Officer, that was exactly what I told them to do.

While they grabbed their weapons to assume guard facing the tent's entrance, I yelled out an order to whoever was listening, "Give me an M4 with some ammo and NODs!"

While bodies moved to get me armed, I was boiling with frustration and confusion. I kicked a metal folding chair, half missing it. The chair went flying in the air, hitting the side of the tent and falling loudly to the floor as I yelled, "How in the hell did the enemy get into our Camp?"

I moved toward the center of the tent where, standing some distance away, I came eye to eye with one of the men in charge of the TOC, the Battle Noncommissioned Officer (NCO), Sergeant First Class Jerry Schools-Butler.

"What happened?" I yelled. "Did the damn guards fall asleep?"

Schools-Butler knew it was rhetorical and didn't answer. His eyes had that "I don't know, Sergeant Major" look.

"Where's that M4 and NODs?" I barked to anyone who was listening.

"He's getting it Sergeant Major," Schools-Butler answered.

It was clear to me that no one knew anything in the Command Center. The look of shock on their faces told me they had no idea what was going on outside, except explosions and gunfire. They were silent. They were in defensive mode.

I could see they were clinging to my every word and watching my every move, as if to say, "What are you going to do to fix this, fearless leader?" I didn't think that I was fearless; I just did not have the time to contemplate fear. I was reacting and executing on autopilot.

Fear would have to wait another day.

With the fury that I had entered the TOC, I had passed Major Kyle Warren, the Brigade Intelligence Officer. Major Warren was from the Sooner state—Oklahoma. Warren had played baseball back home, but wasn't built like a power hitter. He was built more like a guy they would put in the outfield, hoping the ball never comes his way, which explains why I did not notice Warren at first.

Now concerned that this was a coordinated attack, I yelled out frantically to block all the entrances to the TOC. That's when I noticed Warren, who began to hustle a few of the soldiers who were on duty and place them in position to guard the entrances. Three entrances were already blocked with equipment, and now the other entrances were covered by personnel.

Warren had previously served as an Infantry Officer and Platoon leader. Therefore, he understood how his intelligence would be used and was darn good at getting useful intel for us. I knew he would be on top of things.

The TOC was massive, made up of four or five connecting tents. It had more computers and communication equipment than some third-world countries. Map boards covered nearly every wall. As the Command Center, it was also the complex that safeguarded the latest plan to infiltrate Iraq, the pinpoint location of High Pay-off Targets and High Value Targets, and known blacklisted enemy suspects.

A soldier placed my requested M4 in one hand and two full 30-round magazines in the other. I put one magazine in the cargo pocket of my military-issued pants, and I locked and loaded the other magazine into the weapon.

The sound of the bolt going forward, chambering a round into weapon, told me that this time my weapons meant business. I was now ready to go out and do some harm. This was not paint ball. I was sure that someone's son would not be coming back home across the border tonight.

I stuck my arm through the three-point sling and attached the weapon to my body. I secured the NODs, sticking my head through the loop and allowing them to hang in front of me, lying on my upper chest like a necklace. It would have been easier to affix them to my helmet, but I didn't have one.

I made my way to the same door that I came in. The two men who now were guarding the entrance were down in the prone position to obtain a more defensive posture. Warren had given them instructions to halt anyone that came into the tent upon sight. They could now just shoot at anyone who entered, like I had a few minutes earlier.

Before exiting into the vestibule, I confirmed the order by yelling, "Shoot at anyone who looks like the enemy." I knew that was vague, but it was simple. I had no idea when I barked those orders that the enemy was one of our own.

* * *

As Romaine crouched in the vestibule of our tent, looking over his injuries and contemplating his next move, Colonel Hodges was still inside. Unbeknownst to me, as I was darting out of the tent, the Colonel was knocked down from the explosion of the second grenade, and fell back into his sleeping area in the now burning, smoke-filled tent.

At 6'2" and 230 pounds, Colonel Hodges felt as if Larry Csonka had pummeled him. Like me, the Colonel did not hear the thunderous concussion-producing grenade blast, and was certain that a large bodied person had knocked him down.

Now reoriented, the Colonel grabbed his military-issue Beretta 9mm that had served him so well during his 22-year career. Gripping his pistol in his left hand so he could use it if need be, the Colonel made his way through the tent and was headed out through the vestibule when he found Romaine.

"Are you okay?" Hodges asked.

"My hands," Romaine said.

The Colonel looked at Romaine's hands and said, "Oh my God. Your hands look like shit."

They were chewed up from sharp edges of the bullet that had ripped through them. They looked like they had to hurt like hell.

Hodges found Romaine a towel to temporarily wrap his hands and to stop some of the bleeding of his leg. A few minutes later, Romaine was able to break free from our tent and make it to the Texas barriers located 20 feet away.

Believing that we were under a full-fledge attack and that Romaine was stabilized for the moment, the Colonel moved to the tent next door, Tent #2. He heard a commotion and wanted to check on the men.

Colonel Hodges had no idea that it was already under fire.

* * *

The enemy was making quick work of it. In the very short time that it had taken me to get a weapon and ammo, another grenade exploded, now a fourth one, and another shot had been fired.

Now fully equipped with weapons and gear, I exited the vestibule of the TOC and switched on the NODs. Then I placed my right thumb on the selector lever of my M4 and my trigger finger just above the trigger well, pointing in the direction of the barrel.

With my left hand holding the NODs and my right hand holding my assault rifle, I moved in a crouched, low position to reduce the size of my silhouette and make myself harder to hit. I headed straight to our tent, which was still smoking from explosives and fire. Although I couldn't see the smoke, as I got closer I could distinctly smell the two different scents. The combination of the two smells was not pleasant.

I learned quickly that I was not "owning the night" with these NODs. The device needed at least a sliver of light to work. One distant star in the night would help. But none existed tonight.

As I dropped the NODs back to my chest, I could tell that my naked eye was no help either. It was darker than anything I had ever witnessed before.

I moved toward the walkway leading to the tent's entrance to try and locate Romaine and Hodges. They weren't in the vestibule where I had expected them to be. I hadn't stumbled over anything; therefore, they weren't lying on the ground. I couldn't see them and I couldn't smell them.

Other than the grit of the sand on the bottom of my boots scraping against the wood, there wasn't a sound. It was eerie. I was alone out there—nothing moved, no sign of any other life.

No training scenario had prepared me to go up against an enemy like this by myself.

Neither Hodges nor Romaine had called out to challenge me in the dark. So I didn't believe they had been there to hear me. I didn't even hear the low, inarticulate sound of any moaning that Romaine might have made as a result of his injuries. I hoped that meant that they weren't badly injured.

I never uttered a word. They weren't there and I didn't want to alert the enemy of my location. Stealth was of the utmost importance here. I was now trying to sneak up on the enemy. I wanted to surprise, not be surprised.

I left the vestibule and moved back toward the Command Center to get some help to find my desert roommates. I thought there would be success in numbers. While someone looked for them, I would continue to look for the enemy.

I began to wonder if all of those explosions were not grenades. Maybe some were rockets being launched at us.

That thought prompted a couple of key questions: How did the enemy get such great intelligence on us to be able to launch rockets with this type of pinpoint accuracy? If they were in fact rockets, why were we not counter launching our Patriot missiles to intercept them?

The Patriot Batteries were a Division asset. They were placed in strategic locations throughout the desert to counter any rocket threat.

I hustled the next few feet back to the TOC, yelling as I got closer, "It's me! It's me, the Sergeant Major," as if that was the new running password. I wanted to make sure that I wouldn't be shot at as I entered. The last thing I wanted to do was to get ambushed and killed by my own men.

* * *

Since I had last been there to get my ammunition and NODs, Major Warren had taken back control of the Guardsmen under his command. He had given specific instructions to secure the area and its vital information.

Warren then swiftly moved outside and began setting up security around the TOC. As soldiers began to appear from the other various tents in the area of the Command Center, Warren grabbed them and placed them along the Texas barriers that encircled the edifice.

Being a former Infantry enlisted man and an Infantry Lieutenant, his thoughts were focused on security, security, security. "Everything good comes from security and accountability" had been our Commander's mantra.

Based on previous SCUD alerts from the very first of the explosions, those in the TOC initially thought there might have been some type of indirect fire attack with chemicals attached to it. Therefore, they had dawned their protective masks as a precaution, only to later remove them.

Warren was concerned that the TOC as a structure really was not secure. Like the sleeping tents, the Command Center was just a vinyl structure. Therefore, the soldiers could be shot right through the tent without anyone seeing by whom or from where the shots were coming.

As the one responsible for the TOC and its staff, Warren had them power down their computers and systems to prepare to fully secure this information palace. When he stepped outside, he, like most, noticed that the generator light set was not lit. He always saw a blue haze hovering above the generator, exiting its diesel fuel. It projected a shadowy, moonlit haze near the flagpole, and it was not there. The generator was off.

Soldiers approached Warren two at a time, and he placed them throughout the walls of barriers in two-person teams. The Bastogne Brigade was in full-on military defensive mode. Despite the darkness, the four grenades, and two burning tents, our brave men and women were falling into place as our years of military training kicked in. Out of the smoke fell dozens of soldiers who were barely discernable one from the other. Like a well-oiled machine, we were falling into line to face our enemy.

We would later look back and realize that our attacker was likely among these men we were ordering in line. We would discover that we had both armed and trained the man who was now professing to protect us.

CHAPTER 3
Internal Damage

In all of the adrenaline-fueled commotion caused by four grenades and small-weapons fire, it was easy to lose track of what was happening in our dark and dusty corner of Camp Pennsylvania.

After the first two grenades had gone off in Tent #1, I was able to escape that tent into the darkness, only to find that I was ill equipped with an ammo-less gun. Even after racing to the Command Center for lethal reinforcement and night-vision goggles, I still found myself unable to cut through the darkness and the confusion.

Major Romaine was severely injured, and Colonel Hodges was just getting his bearings back when a third grenade was thrown into Tent #2, and a fourth grenade into Tent #3. We had no idea how many attackers were running through the camp, where they were, what weapons they had, or how long they could sustain the attack.

In this one-sided firefight, four grenades would be tossed and several shots would be fired. In the end, two warfighters would be dead and 12 wounded.

However, as Tent #2 came under attack, we did not know any of that.

* * *

Asleep on their thin mattress pads, our neighbors to the immediate north heard the blasts in our tent only 10 feet away. Tent #2 was where all of our Majors were housed, along with a couple of Captains and our two Kuwaiti interpreters.

After hearing the blasts in our tent, the sleeping officers next door began to move quickly, grabbing their uniforms, attempting to get dressed, and lacing up their boots. It was clear that they had no idea that their tent would be next.

Major Shawn Phillips was in Tent #2. He was our logistics officer in the Bastogne Brigade. He had been with us since the previous summer and had proven to be very resourceful. The Major was the one responsible for getting all of us to Kuwait with all the gear we needed to fight the battle in Iraq. Despite all of his planning, he did not realize that we would be facing our own enemy on this side of the Kuwait/Iraq border.

Phillips was awoken by the blast, and was barely up when he heard a shot and Major Romaine cry out in pain. Just across the aisle and to Phillips' left, Captain Townley Hedrick also was shocked awake by the noise. Hedrick stayed down on his mat pad in the prone position waiting for the attackers to come through the door.

Hedrick embodied integrity and moral strength. Hailing from upstate New York in the small town of Wellsville, Hedrick grew up wrestling through high school and all the way to James Madison University. He was a consummate team player, and his toned, medium build showed he was an all-around athlete.

Also in the tent were battle buddies Major Gregory Stone and Captain Mark 'Duke' Wisher. Stone had joined us in Camp Pennsylvania just three weeks before the attack. They were our liaisons between the U.S. Army and the U.S. Air Force. Major Stone was a soft-spoken man with a quiet demeanor, a big heart, and a sharp wit. His buddy, Captain Wisher, struck a sharp contrast with his tall, thin build and a pilot's bravado that he kept hidden behind a smile of sheer confidence.

We needed them on the team to quickly translate Army-speak into Air Force-speak, particularly when we needed to tell their pilots to drop bombs on high priority targets at a moment's notice. Each military service had their own lingo, their own weapon systems, and their own technology. Though the Army could technically communicate with the pilots, it happened at light speed if they heard from one of their own in their own language.

Major Stone had spent his first eight years of active duty in the Air Force as an enlisted man, trained as a Boom Operator on a KC-135, which is basically a flying gas station. After receiving his commission, he became a Weapon Systems Operator in the B-52 Bomber and finally the B-1 Bomber. He left active duty after about 15 years and joined the Air National Guard as a full-time Air Force Liaison Officer, which was his position during our time in Kuwait.

Captain Wisher had served as an F-16 fighter pilot, flying bombing missions over Afghanistan and guarding the Korean

Demilitarized Zone, or DMZ. This mission in the desert was to be his safest yet. He had not expected to see close-quarter combat in this advisory role.

Wisher wasn't one to take chances though. He had taken some time earlier in the evening of March 22 to chat with the Kuwaiti interpreters. They talked for about 15 minutes before Wisher racked out. He couldn't help but to be a little weary of the new guests. He slept with his 9mm Beretta closer than previous nights, just in case they tried anything funny.

After hearing the blasts in neighboring Tent #1, Wisher and Stone had just made it to their feet and had begun to get dressed when the tent flaps in Tent #2 moved. Preceded by the words, "We're under attack," they heard an audible clunk on the wooden floor, followed by the sound of something rolling, scraping along the sandy, wooden floor.

In the span of a second, Wisher remembers thinking, "You know you don't have any training or experience with grenades, but that sounded just like in the movies when a grenade hits and rolls across the floor."

The rolling sound stopped at the foot of Wisher's sleeping bag. He was trapped. He did not have time to rip down the partitions in the tent. He couldn't go to the right because of the tent wall, and the grenade was to his left.

Wisher felt like a cockroach caught in a corner, frantically looking for a hole small enough to squeeze through. He crouched down and turned his right side toward the grenade.

Time was up.

Five seconds is all it takes for a grenade to explode once the pin has been pulled. It exploded between the sleeping bags, five feet away from Wisher and a foot closer to Stone. It was less than an inch from Major Warren's sleeping mat.

Luckily for the Major, he was on the night shift at the TOC.

The tent began to fill with asphyxiating black smoke. With the outside generator out of commission, the only light in the area came from the fires in the tents created by the explosions.

Phillips saw the grenade flash and hit the ground, but not soon enough to clear the area. For that slight hesitation to confirm that he just saw a grenade, Phillips caught two pieces of shrapnel in the thigh.

Hedrick was hit in both feet by shrapnel. Being so close to the impact of the grenade's concussion, he felt as though someone had teed off with a golf club to the bottom of his feet. Confused in the midst of the suffocating smoke, he tended as best he could to his own wounds. He grabbed a poncho liner and wrapped it around his feet. He could feel that they were bleeding, and he was thankful that he couldn't see them.

Trying to connect the dots, Hedrick thought maybe a mortar hit them. As the smoke cleared, he could see that there was no hole in the roof of the tent. He quickly deduced that if it was a grenade then someone would come right in behind it to clear the tent, or maybe they would just shoot through the tent walls. So he stayed down, with his weapon drawn and focused on the tent's entrance.

Major Phillips positioned himself to do the same. While waiting for what seemed like forever for the impeding assault, they heard the fourth and final grenade explode, closely followed by a second gun shot from the tent on the other side of them— Tent #3.

* * *

I busted through the center of the TOC tent flap as if the last explosion had been a foot behind me, stepping over two soldiers lying in the prone position. I found Schools-Butler and summoned him to help me find Hodges and Romaine.

"Roger that Sergeant Major," he quickly replied.

I did not see Warren in the Command Center. As far as I knew, it was only Schools-Butler and me in the fight against an unknown enemy. I believed that we were outnumbered.

Schools-Butler ran to grab his gear so he could begin his search-and-rescue mission of the remaining Command team.

The Battle Captain on duty was our Chemical Officer. He was standing near the map and dry erase boards that covered more than half of a tent wall. The 5-foot-9 Captain, who was 165 pounds on a good day, didn't look afraid, but he was clearly under pressure to sort out the current situation.

I quickly moved past him without bothering to ask if there was an update and continued toward the radios to initiate a call for help.

Schools-Butler and I weren't going to be able to tackle this alone. Right then, I needed manpower, numbers, soldiers. The adrenaline still had me pumped up and energized.

With my throat dry, I grab the radio handset to say, "Any station this net, this is Bastogne 7 . . . we're under attack . . . I say again, we are under attack!"

Lieutenant Colonel (LTC) Chris Hughes, the Commander of 2-327, answered immediately as if he was waiting on me to personally call him.

"This is No Slack 6," he replied, identifying his Battalion.

"Sir," I said, immediately disregarding standard call signs. "I need some damn help over here now!"

"What do you need?"

"I need at least a Squad, no a Platoon. I don't know how many there are or what we're looking for. I haven't been able to ID shit."

"Roger that, they're on the way . . . Do you need anything else?

"Negative. Send them in the vicinity of the TOC."

I had confidence that they could find the Command Center in the dark. I didn't tell him anything about Colonel Hodges or Major Romaine. I didn't have time to get into details of the whole story.

No Slack was located about three-and-a-half football fields away, just past the chow tent. I couldn't wait on them. I would brief them once they got here. Just as I stepped away, headed toward the exit, I heard a call through the radio's speaker.

"Do you need a medevac?" a voice asked, referring to sending support for a Medical Evacuation.

It was a smart Medic at the Aide Station on the Camp. Thank God for him.

"Yes," I said knowing that Romaine was severely injured.

"I'm sending an FLA [Field Litter Ambulance] in the vicinity of the TOC."

"Roger that."

As I rushed to get out of the TOC, I couldn't help but wonder why the Battle Captain failed to initiate those same calls. No one had really reported anything before I made the call saying that we were under attack. I guessed that despite intense training, even the most battle-ready soldier could be shaken by explosions just a few feet away.

I also was still having a hard time understanding how the enemy got past our security. There was no way that all of our soldiers had fallen asleep.

I turned to the Battle Captain and told him, "Call Division and tell them that we're being attacked. We don't have enough information for a SITREP [Situation Report] yet."

"Yes, Sergeant Major," he said.

With these questions and more still nagging at me, I parted the tent flaps to exit once again into the darkness.

* * *

The blast in Tent #2 had thrown Wisher up against the side of the tent. He was dazed from the concussion of the blast. He gained enough of his senses to look at his legs and arms to see if they were still attached. He looked to his left to check on his friend, Stone, who was beside him before the blast.

Stone, a soft-spoken man that no one in the tent had ever heard so much as raise his voice, screamed for help at the top of his lungs. He used every bit of the strength that he had left in his body. Stone had a severe, two-inch hole on the left side of his throat. The blood was squirting across the room from his neck.

Severely injured himself, Wisher put his left arm around Stone's head and neck for support. Wisher then applied direct pressure with his right hand on Stone's neck wound to try to stop the bleeding. After Wisher realized that he didn't have a bandage or compress, and not wanting to remove his hand and release the pressure from Stone's neck, Wisher yelled for a medic, multiple times.

No one came.

Hedrick, whose feet were still throbbing, saw Wisher working on Stone and heard his cry for a medic. He witnessed Stone's horrific neck wound, and the other numerous smaller gashes to his chest and lower extremities made by the shrapnel. Hedrick threw Wisher a T-shirt to help stop Stone's bleeding.

Hedrick then looked to see what he could do to put out the fires still smoldering in Tent #2. He slid his boots onto his wounded feet, sending shooting pains through his body. He knew he couldn't stomp out the fires with his wounds, so he grabbed an MRE box and used it to put out one of the fires.

Phillips worked to put out another fire still burning in Tent #2, which was in the area where the chaplain and the interpreters had been staying. They were gone.

Major Verner Kiernan, the Brigade Fire Support Officer, who was housed in Tent #2 also heard Wisher's calls for help. Kiernan was one of the lucky ones who had escaped being injured by the grenade blast. He was now returning to help his comrades.

The smoke was beginning to suffocate Wisher. Hell bent on saving Stone, Wisher ignored his own injuries. Eventually, he noticed the stream of blood trickling down his own arm. He also saw that the right side of his t-shirt and his right pant leg were soaked in blood.

Stone's gasps for air seized Wisher's attention away from his own injuries.

"Stay with me . . . you're going to be okay," Wisher told Stone. But it was too late. Stone's eyes rolled back into his head as he began to lose consciousness.

Wisher took yet another T-shirt and applied it to Stone's neck wound to help stop the persistent blood loss, but Wisher was losing strength. Kiernan took over applying pressure to the dressing on Stone's neck. It was not looking good.

* * *

With Tents #1 and #2 ablaze, the 14 Captains and two Lieutenants housed in Tent #3 were next on the enemy's hit list.

Hearing the commotion from the blasts in the two nearby tents, the officers were roused from their sleep. They stared at each other momentarily to confirm what they had just heard, then quickly made the decision to get out of the tent and get into the bunkers that were positioned throughout the Brigade Headquarters. They scrambled in the dark to find any part of their uniform, to get dressed, to locate their gear, and to leave.

Assistant Intelligence Officer, Captain Chris Seifert, was among the Tent #3 soldiers scrambling to aid in the attack. They had no idea what had happened, or what lay in wait for them.

Seifert was an affable guy, proud to hail from the small, rural community of Williams Township, PA. Roughly four months before our deployment, Chris and Terri Seifert had introduced the newest member of their family, a son. This would be the Captain's first experience with combat, and he felt ready to head into battle.

Seifert was the first dressed in Tent #3 and managed to get his helmet and vest on and secured, with his weapon in hand, before he exited the tent. He hustled in the direction of the TOC where his immediate boss, Warren, was taking control.

As he emerged from the tent, he paused for a moment to orient himself. Surprised to find zero illumination, Seifert wondered what had happened to the generator's lights.

Before he could make it past the Texas barriers just outside the tents, someone ran up behind Seifert, placed the barrel of his weapon just a few inches from the small of Seifert's back, pulled the trigger, and continued running into the dark.

The round struck Seifert just below the protection of the sappy plate in his armored vest. He fell to the ground face down, yelling from the pain.

First Sergeant Rod Stevenson had just exited out of Tent #4 which housed the non-commissioned officers. Immediately after his eyes adjusted to the dark, Stevenson heard the shot.

Stevenson had been with the Bastogne Brigade since December 1999. I handpicked him from a pool of about 15 First Sergeants to be an integral part of the headquarters team as our fearless Company First Sergeant. I needed someone who was not intimidated by the top brass, and who could back me up as a leader among our Non-Commissioned Officer corps.

A towering 6-feet and 250 pounds, Stevenson was not afraid of much. So it was no surprise that he was one of the first out of the noncom tent.

The first thing Stevenson saw as his eyes adjusted was Seifert's collapse, and someone running away.

He sprinted to Seifert, and heard only a barely audible murmur. Stevenson saw Seifert had been shot in the back. He gently turned him over, praying that he saw an exit wound. But there was none.

No exit wound meant that the round stayed inside the body, with the potential to bounce left and right like a pinball, cutting through vital organs with its razor sharp edges.

Staff Sergeant Matt Sawyer was right behind Stevenson out of Tent #4. He quickly moved in on Seifert. He and Stevenson worked feverishly, trying to stop the bleeding with direct pressure.

Sawyer was smaller than Stevenson, but just as tough. The 5-foot-5, 140-pound career soldier was well trained and immediately focused on helping out the injured, starting with Seifert.

Colonel Hodges, who was now free from the blinding smoke in Tent #1, joined the two men with Seifert, providing the best first responder aid and comfort that they could.

Hodges leaned down to talk to Seifert, "Chris, are you okay?"

"Yes, but my back hurts," Seifert replied. Hodges had no idea how badly his soldier was injured.

* * *

Before the first grenade was thrown, the five-man team in charge of planning our entry into Iraq—Major Pat Frank and Captains Craig Butera, Kevin Williams, Mike Sabatini, and Tony Jones—took off early. They had finalized the plans for our imminent invasion into Iraq. They had put in a lot of late nights and long hours, and were headed to a much-needed shower.

Before heading to the showers, the team went back to their tents to grab their flip-flops, towels, and shave kits, the Major to Tent #2 and the Captains to Tent #3.

They all enjoyed a stress-free shower knowing that for once they didn't have to hurry back to work. Butera, who had entered the shower last, lathered up his head with shaving cream in preparation to style a new bald look for the Iraqi border crossing.

Most of the shower crew had finished and were exiting the shower trailer when the explosions began.

All of these guys, maybe with the exception of Jones, were practical jokers. So when Butera, who was the last one out of the showers, heard a loud noise and felt something shake, he immediately thought that it was his turn to be the brunt of a joke. He stopped shaving and leaned in to focus on the noise.

Just when he did, Williams burst back in the trailer, "Dude, something's going on. You gotta get outta here."

With a half-shaven head, Butera, quickly jumped out of the shower, put on his T-shirt and his Desert Camouflage Uniform, or DCUs. He then threw on his unlaced boots and grabbed his weapon. The team hustled toward their tents to get the rest of their gear. Jones was the first one back to Tent #3 after what would be the final explosion, and made it in just as Seifert was walking out, headed toward his unfathomable fate.

Following the explosion in the tent next to his, Tent #2, Captain Dexter McClendon, who slept near the back of the tent, immediately gave up on making it out the front to see what the flurry of activity was about. He used his bayonet to cut his way out of the heavily blocked rear of the tent.

Captain Ramon Rubucaba made his way down the aisle and was headed out of Tent #3. He would be the last one to leave this tent, just before the fourth and final grenade would be tossed.

Rubucaba kept moving toward the vestibule and crashed

smack dab into a soldier who was coming into the tent. Barely registering the incident in the chaos, he moved to the side and proceeded toward the bunker.

We later realized that this was likely the first face-to-face contact we would have with our attacker—Hasan Akbar.

CHAPTER 4
Taking Stock

The all-male CBS news crew was housed in Tent #7, separated from the female soldiers by a piece of plywood and from the action by the length of just one tent.

Reporter Mark Strassmann and cameraman Don Lee, along with their military point man, Lieutenant Colonel (LTC) Jim Lacey of the Army Reserve, were all up after the first grenades went off. They were scrambling to get out of the tent as the shots were fired and the other grenades were tossed.

Shrapnel ripped through the back of Tent #2, flying into the back of the media's tent. The blast debris injured only one of the female soldiers, with a flesh wound to the leg.

As the news crew took cover in a nearby bunker, they continued to try and figure out exactly what was happening.

From the bunker, the media could hear the anxious sounds of injured soldiers, the panicked yells for a medic, and the booming commands from leaders as they placed security around the perimeter. LTC Jim Lacey was one of those leaders.

Lacy was a big man at 6'3, 240 pounds, who had been a former Infantry Company Commander in the Bastogne Brigade in the mid-eighties, serving along with Hodges. And what he realized was missing from the scene were leaders establishing security around the perimeter, so he traded his *Time Magazine* ballpoint pen for an Army M4 rifle and switched into full military mode in an attempt to assist.

Because no one had taken charge in the rear half of the Brigade area, Lacey started setting in a perimeter there. He grabbed a Sergeant and introduced himself using his military rank. "I'm Colonel Lacey, (short for LTC), go find two other NCOs and bring them to me." The Sergeant was startled for a moment when he looked up at Lacy wearing civilian clothes and holding a military assault rifle. Convinced that he really was a Colonel, he said, "Yes sir," and within a minute he returned with two more men.

Lacey assigned them different sectors and told them to grab soldiers by pairs to fill in the perimeter. He walked the line calming nervous soldiers, pointing out directions of where not to shoot, and emphasizing not to fire unless fired upon. Assured that everything was under control, he left the two senior Sergeants in charge.

Meanwhile, despite the danger, Strassmann and Lee ran from the bunker where the media crew was grouped and headed toward the tents in the front row to see what was happening on the battlefield. Lee, a long-time news veteran with a friendly demeanor, got his camera fired up and began filming. Strassmann, first-time war correspondent who was honored (and anxious) to have the opportunity to tell the story from the front lines, stuck his head into one of the smoldering tents and got a full nose of cordite that was still lingering in the air.

While CBS was bunking on our side of Camp Pennsylvania, Sky TV was on the other side of it. Unfortunately for them, they were now on lockdown. As a result, the Sky TV crew was blocked from the action, giving Mark, Don, and CBS an exclusive, front-row seat.

While Don captured footage of our wounded being loaded onto litters, Mark got on his satellite phone to break the urgent news to Dan Rather.

Millions of viewers tuned into the annual CBS basketball thriller March Madness were going to be preempted with the first news report from the two-day-old war effort. It would be the first report since the failed attempt on Saddam's life, with the torrential downpour of bombs on Baghdad, and the first report of any attack on American soldiers since the war started.

* * *

As CBS news began their reporting from the front lines, we were feverishly working to uncover the source of the attack and to take care of our wounded. We still had no idea if the attack had just begun or was already over.

While we were assessing the situation, SCUD alarms were going off signaling incoming air attacks. Some of our wounded thought they saw Tracer fire. We did witness one of our Patriot missiles fired, but in the darkness we could not be sure exactly what was going in or going out.

51

All we knew for sure was that the injuries were piling up.

Tent #2 was the hardest hit. Most of its 11 inhabitants had retired for the night. Tent #3 had 16 men bunking there, but several of them had hit the showers or were still on duty. My tent, Tent #1, had only three players.

It was Tent #2 where our team began to house the wounded, despite the fact that it was still smoldering from the grenade blast. Many of the men could not be moved very far due to their injuries. So Tent #2 became our triage center as we waited for help to arrive.

* * *

The bloodied and determined Major Romaine fled the vestibule of Tent #1 where he had been shot trying to escape the two grenades that had been tossed under our tent flaps. He was seeking cover along the Texas barriers, heading toward Tents #2 and #3 when he stumbled upon Lieutenant Gian Armosolo.

It was the first time that Romaine realized others were injured. Armosolo, a slight, young Lieutenant who looked every bit of 17 years old and worked with logistics, received a shrapnel wound to his leg as he lay in bed in Tent #3. He was screaming from the heat and pain of his wound as blood spurted out of his knee.

Romaine helped steer Armosolo back to Tent #2 where the makeshift triage had begun. First Sergeant Stevenson was also there, working with the wounded.

Stevenson was in full multi-task, guru mode. He was overseeing the search for the enemy by other soldiers while also focusing on getting the wounded treated and evacuated out of the area.

With Armosolo at his side, Romaine asked Stevenson where to take the wounded. Stevenson gestured toward Tent #2, despite the fact that portions of it were still on fire. Bleeding pretty steadily from his own hand wounds, Romaine staggered his way into the tent.

Captain Hedrick was already in the tent and helped Romaine sit on his tentmate Warren's tough box, right beside where the grenade had exploded.

Major Phillips quickly removed Romaine's pistol from his weak and bloodied hands.

Focused on Romaine's unsightly hands, Hedrick wrapped them with a towel. The look on Hedrick's face told Romaine how bad his hands were.

"Well, somebody better take a look at my leg too," Romaine said.

Hedrick found another towel to wrap the injured leg. As he got some temporary patch work, Romaine looked across the tent and saw the combat life savers still working frantically on Stone's profusely bleeding neck wounds.

Hedrick was beginning to feel trapped inside the smoky tent. Even though he knew his fellow soldiers were getting the care they needed, Hedrick still felt guilty about leaving Romaine and the others in the tent as he left to get some air.

He had a very uneasy, even fearful, feeling that Iraqi soldiers were going to raid the tent at any moment. At least from the outside, Hedrick believed he would be able to prevent the Iraqi soldiers from coming in, therefore providing protection for those remaining inside the tent. He had no idea that most of the space in front of the tents was secured and protected already.

Captain Wisher, who was being treated for his own wounds, stopped Hedrick as he was leaving the Tent #2 triage, and asked him to help with Stone. Knowing the severity of the injuries, Hedrick hung his head and said, "I have no help to give."

* * *

Captain Gregory Holden, Company Commander for the Headquarters Company of the Bastogne Brigade, was hit hard in the Tent #3 blast. He attempted to administer first aid to himself as soon as he realized no medic was coming.

An intelligence officer and a fellow avid Ohio State Buckeye fan, Holden had joined the brigade about a year earlier. We had bonded quickly in those early days and became a great team. I imparted what knowledge I had to help him effectively run the day-to-day operations of the company at Fort Campbell, which in turn allowed the Brigade Commander to command.

He had been the first of our team to arrive at Camp Pennsylvania just a few weeks earlier. It was his job to inventory and sign for the camp's belongings and designate where the company would live when we arrived in our new, sandy quarters.

Now, in the aftermath of the grenade blasts, Holden was frustrated that he could not locate everything he needed right when he needed it.

Holden searched every pouch on his vest looking for a first-aid pressure bandage. The blast ripped almost everything off of his body armor. Knowing exactly where everything was located just seconds earlier, he now could not find his first aid kit. Nothing was there. His ammo pouches and magazines were all gone.

He managed to remove his heavy body armor, enabling him to breathe and think more clearly.

Jones, who was recovering from his own minor injuries, ignored his wounds to help Holden who had taken the brunt of the blast. Holden's body position had prevented Jones from being injured worse than he was. Jones tried to pick up Holden to carry him outside of the tent for treatment and to be assessed priority for transport by the Field Litter Ambulance.

As Jones lifted Holden up on his shoulder, Holden felt excruciating pain. The foot on his injured leg, though attached, was shattered. His left foot just dangled, flopping like a chicken with his head half cut off. Holden's yell let Jones know that something was terribly wrong and that lifting him was a bad idea.

Two first responders, Captains Roberts and Sabatini, heard Holden's cry for help and assisted.

Now that Holden's body armor was off, he felt some discomfort in his abdominal area. He rubbed his hand over the area and found that his finger slid right into a hole in his stomach. He also realized that his left hand, although fully functioning, was injured. The shrapnel had cut through most of it and the tendons and bones were visible.

His first responders helped him lie down and elevated his injured leg. It was then that Holden said he could see that his foot was partially detached from his leg, flopping to the side and hanging on by just tendons. The left knee was facing skyward, and the toe of his foot was pointing to the floor. Every time they would stop the bleeding in one part of the leg, it would leak from a different spot.

Sawyer walked in on the officers trying to help Holden. He made a quick assessment and realized that it was too late for pressure dressings. Holden had lost a lot of blood. Sawyer started applying a tourniquet of his own belt and a piece of a cot that was left behind. He applied the tourniquet to Holden's leg as high as he could get it, which was just below Holden's groin. Sawyer then tied the other end of the cot bar off at Holden's chest. It hurt like hell, but Holden knew that it was saving his life.

Still coherent, Holden knew that a tourniquet was a serious and scary procedure, if not managed properly. As timing was of the utmost of importance, Holden took on the task of being his own timekeeper. After all, it was his leg at stake.

After roughly 10 minutes, Holden called out for the tourniquet to be loosened. No one wanted to loosen it for fear that it wasn't time. To further complicate matters, Holden thought one of his lungs had collapsed because he was having a terrible time trying to breathe. The smoke inhaled from the grenade and the sheer exhaustion from the loss of blood and pain induced by his wounds were becoming too much for him.

LTC Lacey made his way to the bloody tents, carrying out some of the wounded on litters, Stone being one of them. He stood over Holden armed with an M4 assault rifle he had been able to procure. However, it didn't have a magazine; rendering it as worthless as my 9mm was to me. Holden took notice that Lacey was fine and that most of his soldiers appeared to be uninjured.

As Holden's soldiers viewed their beloved Company Commander's wounds, they could not hide their expressions of horror and shock.

Holden felt the huge crush to his leader ego, feeling that he had let his soldiers down. As if it were his idea to be blown up!

* * *

When the initial grenades exploded, Jeanette Smith, a Specialist 4 (SPC 4) from Tent 7, was told to go to a bunker. During her sprint to the bunker, she too heard cries for help and ascended upon the tents of injured soldiers instead. 'Smitty' as I referred to her, had blond hair with a fair complexion, and stood 5'4. She was 110 pounds at best, and a fellow Buckeye as well.

She entered Tent 3 and came across a wounded soldier who was in hysterical shock. She held his hand while viewing his mangled body. He was afraid of dying and begged her not to leave him. "You're not going to die, you're not going to die," she assured him. "Tell me about your family, tell me about your kids," she offered, doing her best to get his mind off the reality of his circumstances while someone else bandaged up his wounds.

As he began to calm, SPC 4 Smith was summoned to retrieve more medical supplies. She recalled the combat lifesaver bag in her Hummer, and as she gathered steam to run to her truck, a soldier grabbed her by the collar of her jacket and jerked her backwards. "Where the hell are you going?" he asked, frustrated that she would put herself in harm's way. "I need to go get my combat lifesaver bag," she insisted. "Ok, go, hurry up." Without an armored vest or helmet, and with total disregard for her own safety, she ran outside of the protection of the perimeter to her Hummer to get the supplies they so desperately needed.

Returning safely with the bag, Smitty pushed Lacey out of the way from where he was comforting Stone and began assisting with pressure dressings to Stone's injuries.

The team of medics and first responders set up and ran the perfect casualty collection point that permitted a smooth ground evacuation to the aid station. They triaged the wounded, which enabled them to be put on the correct litters, prioritizing the evacuation out of the danger zone.

Because we never knew when we might be called upon to help save a life, several of the soldiers in the Company were combat lifesaver qualified. Their training paid heavy dividends that night. Those combat lifesavers, like SPC 4 Smith and a group of Officers, NCOs, and soldiers, worked as a team to provide vital medical care.

Without a doubt those measures helped to save and sustain lives and limbs. While not the typical job of an Officer, they really stepped up. Their selfless actions that night would shape and mold how they would lead soldiers and civilians alike for the rest of their lives.

* * *

Just on the other side of the Texas barrier from the tents, the outside light set came on as the power to the generator was finally restored. The light provided immense help in treating the casualties. We had been without lights for the first 10-15 minutes of the ordeal; now, we could move faster and be more efficient in our search for the enemy.

We had two medevac, short for "medical evacuation," helicopters en route. Once loaded, they had a three-minute flight to the closest field hospital, known as a Combat Support Hospital, or CSH.

After a quick medical priority assessment, Stone was the first to be loaded onto the field ambulance, headed for the first flight out. Holden was close behind.

While waiting for everyone to be loaded into the ambulance, the Chaplain's assistant Staff Sergeant Mark Grimsley decided to provide some assurance to the wounded. He was popular among the crew. It was his first tour of combat duty, and we knew he would do anything for us. The only problem was that he wasn't sure what to do.

Grimsley came upon Holden and started with the standard verbiage from a basic training first-aid class. He was at Holden's side reciting, "Hey soldier, I'm the Chaplain's assistant, you're going to be all right, you're going to be okay . . . everything is taken care of"—all the while never once looking at Holden to acknowledge who he was.

Holden, low on blood but still full of spunk, grabbed Grimsley's shirt, pulled him forward, and said, "Sergeant Grimsley, I'm your Company Commander. I know who the hell you are, and you know who I am. Look at me!"

The combat lifesavers stabilized Seifert enough to load him on a manual military stretcher, or a litter. He continued to lose a lot of blood as he was rushed to the waiting medevac. Wisher was loaded immediately behind him.

Romaine was carried on a litter right behind them both, headed for the camp aid station where he would wait for the second airlift to the field hospital. Soon after he was loaded, he noticed that he was beside Seifert, who was moaning from the pain. He tried to comfort his comrade by saying, "You're going to be all right."

Seifert was incoherent at that point and did not respond.

* * *

The medevac aircraft was having problems locating the Pick-Up Zone.

The Air NCO, Tom Air-Butler, overheard the confusion over the radio. Having identified the pick-up location, he fired a flare over the area to identify it as the Pick-Up Zone. This enabled the aircraft to find a suitable location to land in close proximity to the camp aid station.

Air-Butler, the quick-witted, steely-eyed veteran leader, had wondered what the confusion was all about. In his mind, we were in the desert and with the exception of the tents' location, the whole Camp was a Pick-Up Zone.

His vector method worked. As the night began to chill the air, the birds landed and the casualties were loaded.

The first helicopter came in and the most critical patients—Stone and Holden—were loaded up for the short flight to the closest Combat Support Hospital about two kilometers away.

Once on the medevac bird, Holden's litter began to fill up with blood. He had lost a lot already and was lying in a puddle of it. He looked up and saw that more was pouring down from the litter above him.

It was Stone's litter.

The flight took off and landed at the field hospital in no time. As they came off the medevac, the floor of the helicopter was full of blood. Holden began to question its origin, knowing that some had leaked down onto his litter; he was not sure if all of it was his or not.

* * *

The second medevac bird landed just as the first one took off.

Now it was Seifert's turn to be loaded. He didn't make the first flight because the medical personnel at the camp aid station were still trying to stabilize him. Romaine and Wisher were quickly loaded after Seifert, followed by Armosolo. The second medevac flight was up and gone for what was expected to be a three-minute trip.

* * *

The closest field hospital staff was fully prepared for the first flight. The floodlights were shining at the entrance path from the helicopter to the emergency room door. The doctors separated the casualties with each doctor taking one patient to prepare for surgery.

The medical staff immediately hooked up an IV and started cutting Holden's uniform off. He now could see a little more of his injured foot. The bones were protruding out the side from the skin, but the foot was still attached. As he assessed the damage, his oxygen turned on. He was immediately knocked out and wheeled into surgery.

Stone, the most gravely injured of the three in the first medevac, was also whisked away into surgery.

* * *

As the first bird was unloaded and the second one began its descent, a loud explosion and a huge fireball appeared in the sky above Camp Pennsylvania.

A Patriot missile had been fired at a flying object headed toward our side of the camp. We had many SCUD alerts in the past that were unfounded; this was the first time that something had been launched in response.

With the earlier siren alert for a SCUD, the sounds of combat on the ground, and now an air attack, those of us on the ground were worried that we had neither the time nor the assets to combat all three threats at once.

We stared at the fireball as it headed in our direction.

* * *

The Crew Chief from the second medevac helicopter knelt down next to Romaine and said, "We'll be down in just a second, you're doing alright?"

Romaine barely said he was okay when the Crew Chief came back and said, "We didn't get approval to land. We cannot land. We have to go somewhere else."

Romaine began thinking to himself, "How far do we have to go because my buddy Seifert is not doing so well over here."

Romaine felt fine. He was stable, he wasn't cold, and nothing really even hurt. It was the magic of morphine. But he could hear Seifert moaning. Romaine knew that his buddy wasn't doing very well. It was imperative that they get him somewhere, quickly.

At the exact moment the pilots prepared to sit the bird down at the nearby field hospital, the Patriot missile was fired at the potential SCUD.

The medevac had to divert. Substantial and crucial life-saving minutes were lost due to the diversion to a different combat hospital in Southern Kuwait.

* * *

The pilots of the second medevac scurried at a pace faster than was normally permitted in order to get Seifert, Wisher, Romaine, and Armosolo to the hospital in Southern Kuwait as quickly as possible.

The medical staff triaged the victims in seconds and quickly separated Romaine from Seifert.

Assuming that all patients were taken to the same operating room, Romaine didn't know if the triage had separated them or if Seifert had died from his wounds.

Romaine was quickly wheeled toward the operating room through what seemed like miles of vestibules in a tent. It was freezing cold. He didn't know if it was actually the cold temperature or the blood loss that made him feel the air so strongly.

They went up and down small slopes and made numerous turns before arriving in a well-lit room. The medical personnel immediately start cutting off Romaine's uniform. They grabbed his hand and poured bottles of sterile water on it so that they could see exactly where the wounds were.

The Doctor wanted to cut off Romaine's wedding ring, but he yelled back, "There's no way! I'm not in any hurry, you can get it off." The Doctor tried different lubricants until the ring finally came off. Then—and only then—did Romaine allow them to put him under and start the surgery.

As Romaine was being prepped for surgery, Seifert was already in the ER being stabilized for surgery. Wisher and Armosolo were treated for their wounds and awaited the next leg of their journey. They hoped to see Romaine and Seifert on that next leg, the flight to Germany.

* * *

As our comrades were being treated, the rest of us were left to discover what happened. We were feverishly working to uncover the cause and to stop the enemy at all costs.

CHAPTER 5
The Timeline – Looking Back

This chart marks the timeline of events to this point, and the following diagrams show the path of Akbar with the grenades.

March 23, 2003

CHART 1 - Timeline - 23 March 2003

0001	hrs	Tiger Woods tees off on the 9th hole of the Bay Hill Invitaional
0106	hrs	Incendiary grenade rolls into Tent #1
0108	hrs	Fragmentary grenade rolls into Tent #1
0108.5	hrs	Frag grenade explodes injuring Hodges
0111	hrs	Romaine is shot

0112	hrs	2nd Frag grenade rolls into Tent #2
0112.5	hrs	2nd Frag grenade explodes injuring Phillips, Hedrick, Wisher, Stone, and Lamb
0113	hrs	3rd Frag grenade rolls into Tent #3
0113.5	hrs	3rd Frag grenade explodes injuring Holden, Bacon, Armosolo, and Jones
0113.8	hrs	Seifert is shot
0114	hrs	First responders assist casualties, triage begins, transport to FLA
0130	hrs	FLA transports casualties to Camp Aid Station
0145	hrs	First medevac Bird flies casualties to local CSH, two minutes away
0150	hrs	Second medevac Bird flies casualties to local CSH, two minutes away
0151	hrs	Patriot shoots down British Tornado aircraft
0152	hrs	Second medevac Bird aborts, flies to new CSH, 15-20 minutes away

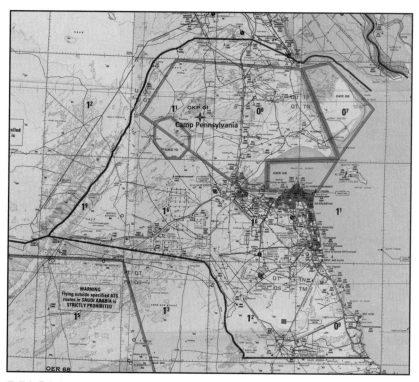

DIAGRAM 1 – Location of Camp Pennsylvania near Kuwait/Iraq Border

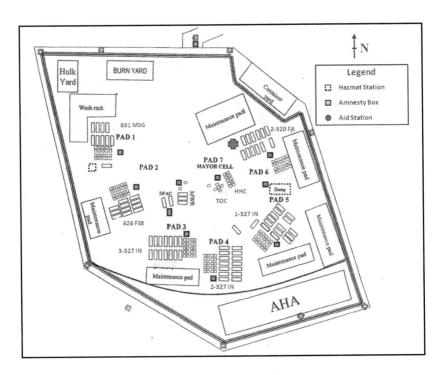

DIAGRAM 2 – Layout of Camp Pennsylvania

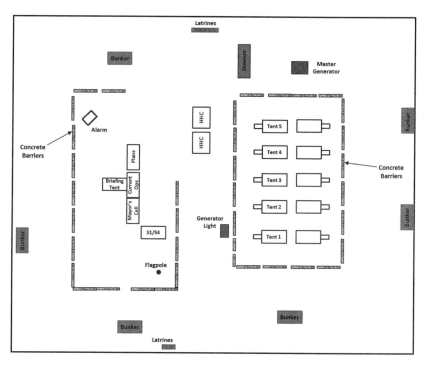

DIAGRAM 3 – Brigade Headquarters Area

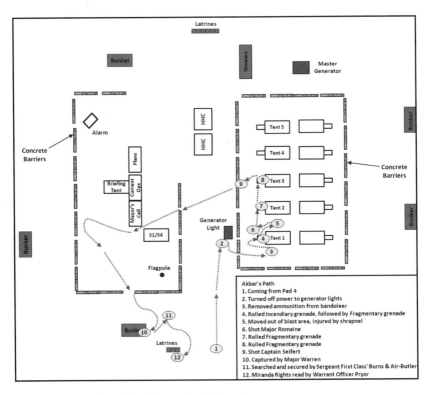

Akbar's Path
1. Coming from Pad 4
2. Turned off power to generator lights
3. Removed ammunition from bandoleer
4. Rolled Incendiary grenade, followed by Fragmentary grenade
5. Moved out of blast area, injured by shrapnel
6. Shot Major Romaine
7. Rolled Fragmentary grenade
8. Rolled Fragmentary grenade
9. Shot Captain Seifert
10. Captured by Major Warren
11. Searched and secured by Sergeant First Class' Burns & Air-Butler
12. Miranda Rights read by Warrant Officer Pryor

DIAGRAM 4 – Akbar's Path of Attack

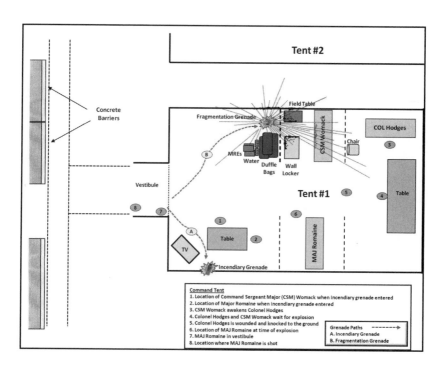

DIAGRAM 5 – Tent #1 with Location of Occupants

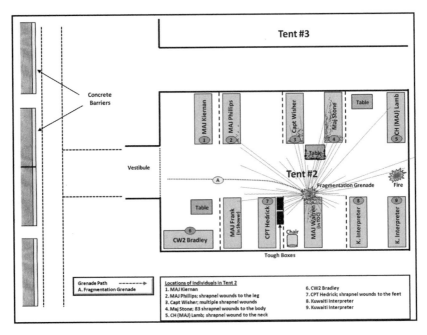

DIAGRAM 6 – Tent #2 with Location of Occupants

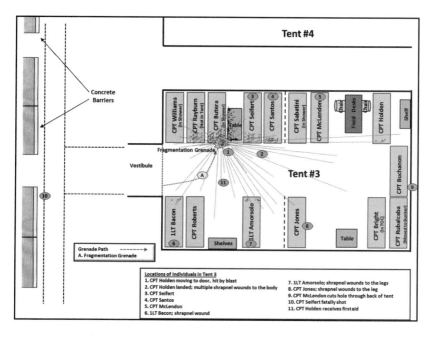

DIAGRAM 7 – Tent #3 with Location of Occupants

SECTION II
ENEMY ON THE LOOSE

CHAPTER 6
The Search

With the wounded medevac'd to the Combat Support Hospitals, the rest of us were left wondering where we were in this battle—beginning, middle, or end.

Who was the enemy? How many were there? What was their goal and what was their capability?

We began to assess the damage, evaluate our options, and for the first time, consider that the attacker was within our ranks.

* * *

As I entered the Command Center, my eyes had a hard time adjusting. The light seemed brighter this time. I turned my head from the lights to rub my eyes and adjust my vision.

When I opened my eyes again, I could see that the center was flowing with people. The volume level was high with a lot of ambient chatter. I couldn't really make out what anyone was saying.

I made my way through the tent to the center where I found the NCO in charge, Sergeant Schools-Butler.

"Where's the Colonel?" I asked, as I scanned the room from left to right.

"Right there," he said, pointing to Colonel Hodges who was sitting directly behind me, about two feet away.

I turned to my rear to see the Colonel sitting in a chair with a soldier on either side of him. I immediately noticed his blood-soaked trousers and his arm in a sling. I walked over to him bending down to his eye level.

"You knocked me down," he said, staring blankly into my eyes.

It took me a second to understand what he meant. The last time I saw my Commander was when we started to run together down the aisle of the tent to escape that first smoking grenade. He had disappeared from my side somewhere between the second grenade blast and my exit from the tent. I had no recollection of running into anything or anyone at all during my exit.

"It wasn't me," I replied with confidence. "It had to be something else."

As I squatted eye-level with the Colonel, I could see his wounds more clearly.

"Are you all right?" I asked.

"Yeah, my arm is sore," he said. He gestured slightly showing me the sling that was keeping his bandaged forearm stable and secure.

"This other blood is the XO's," Colonel Hodges said, referring to our third tentmate, Major Romaine.

"What the hell happened?" I asked. This was the first time I was alerted to the severity of Romaine's injuries.

"We're still trying to figure that out," the Colonel said. "Somehow the enemy got into our camp."

Just then Schools-Butler walked over and interrupted our conversation.

"The XO is on the medevac Sergeant Major," he said.

"Thanks," I said to the Sergeant, who turned and left to gather more intel on our wounded and whom the enemy could be.

"He was pretty banged up," Hodges said of Romaine. He hung his head as he thought about the impact of the past hour.

To the Colonel's left was an Army Specialist who was there to help him as needed. To his right was a soldier with his head down so low I couldn't see his face. He wore a black fleece jacket like mine with no nametag on it, so I wasn't sure exactly who it was. He had no visible injuries, no blood, but you could tell that he was completely devastated.

I tried to look into his face, tried to find his eyes. But he continued to keep his focus on the floor. I asked him if he was okay. He made a small, undistinguishable gesture, but never moved his lips. It was definitely something he just couldn't describe at the time.

Posttraumatic stress can happen fast, and he appeared to have an early case.

* * *

Colonel Hodges somehow found the energy to tie his boots, stand up, and focus on our next steps. He was at the radios and map boards in the Command Center scanning every scrap of info available, observing everyone in the TOC with an eagle eye. He picked up a handset and spoke to a caller in hushed, urgent tones.

He walked over to me after hanging up, pulled me to the side, and said that he asked LTC Hughes to come to the TOC. Hodges said he was not feeling very well, so he wanted Hughes on deck in case he took a turn for the worse. Luckily for us all, Hodges only strengthened over time, and Hughes was able to return to his duties.

He walked with me back to where the staff had gathered. We all stood wide-eyed, waiting for him to speak. This was the first time since the first grenade was tossed that our injured Commander was talking to us. We were all ears; no one dared speak.

"We need to make a net call to all of our units and get accountability of our personnel," the Colonel said as he took charge of the room.

Major Frank jumped on the net call command right away and followed the order.

"I don't understand how the enemy got past our security," I said, not really expecting a response. I believe I spoke for many of us who were still confused about what exactly had just happened.

I continued, "Something had to have changed on the camp."

Major Warren responded, saying, "We had a couple of Kuwaiti interpreters come in last night."

"That's it!" I said, accusing them immediately. I became silent as I considered that they were the only change to the Camp. It had to be them, I thought.

"I'll send Sergeant Air-Butler to find them," Warren said. He knew that Air-Butler had picked the interpreters up and brought them to the camp. Therefore, Air-Butler knew who they were and what they looked like.

As the conversation progressed, I noticed that Colonel Hodges' voice became less audible as he talked to us. He was fading fast. The effects of the concussion from the grenade caused the slightest Traumatic Brain Injury and appeared to be setting in. I suggested to him that he might want to sit down. He found a chair and sat right there in the middle of all of the operational action, leaving us to carry out his orders.

* * *

Major Warren headed toward the exit of the tent, and I was right behind him. As I walked out, I looked around at my Soldiers to gauge their state of mind. The chaos was far from over, and I needed to understand how they were affected.

I was glad to see that they were moving like little bees, hustling from point A to point B, simply doing their jobs— searching and securing the area.

As I exited the TOC tent into the night, I quickly scanned the inside perimeter to determine how well our defense was set up. I was glad to see dozens of soldiers lying prone or on one knee, facing outward toward the enemy.

Lacey had also returned to check on the perimeter he initially established. He walked down the line, position-by-position, reiterating who he was to the different soldiers now in place. "Someone's coming, should I shoot?" a soldier asked him. "No shooting, put your weapons on safe," he shouted loudly so that everyone on the line could hear him.

Though it was dark across the Camp, the restored light near our smoldering tents coupled with the illumination from a light just west of the TOC, gave our security some visibility into the surrounding area. At least we could positively identify people as friend or foe when they approached our Command Center.

Despite the First Sergeant's efforts in training his soldiers, he could never be too careful when it came to avoiding fratricide. And Warren was right, they always faced the possibility that someone could get anxious, thinking that they saw something that was not there, and prematurely pull the trigger. Once that happened, all hell could break loose with friendly shooting friendly. That would add even more to the already chaotic situation.

The soldier's level of training was confirmed to me when Sergeant First Class Tom Burns, one the most compassionate and understanding guys on the team, challenged me after I had exited the TOC earlier in the pitch dark. I had no fear of accidental friendly fire.

Now satisfied that we were doing the right thing, I moved to the area on the other side of the TOC where the vehicles were parked. I ran into First Sergeant Stevenson.

"How are you doing?" I asked him.

"I'm all right, but this is messed up," Stevenson said. He gave me an update on the security, and how well the medical evacuation went. I told him to get accountability and send it to the Command Center. He had heard the net call and said that he was pretty close to having that complete.

"What the hell happened to Sergeant Major?" Stevenson said with total frustration.

"I don't know man," I said. "We're still trying to figure that out."

It was almost 0200 hours, more than 50 minutes after the first grenade went off, and we were no closer to identifying the enemy embedded in our ranks.

* * *

I ran into Command Sergeant Major Richard Montcalm, the Command Sergeant Major for 2-327 No Slack, as I walked through the center of our Headquarters on my way back toward our tents to get the latest update on the situation.

The Sergeant Major and I met about two years before when he had taken the reins from me, as the No Slack Command Sergeant Major, shortly after I accepted the position as the Bastogne Brigade Command Sergeant Major. This wasn't his first tour in No Slack. In 1998, he left No Slack for a new assignment in a different geographical location. When that assignment ended in 2001, he was reassigned back to No Slack in a new position. I hadn't seen him since our last Sergeant Majors meeting, three days earlier.

My first thought was, "What the heck is he doing way over here?" I soon realized that I should have fully expected him to be there, right smack dab in the middle of the action. Lauded for having knowledge of more gadgets than "Get Smart," Montcalm was always where the action was. He no doubt accompanied the No Slack Infantry that I had so desperately summoned earlier from LTC Hughes.

Montcalm, a burly warfighter with a brown high-and-tight head of hair and a stern smile, approached me and told me he had relieved Lacey of his perimeter duties and directed his guys to secure the area to the left, right, and rear of our still-smoldering sleeping tents. He also was forming and sending out patrols to search beyond those areas for the elusive enemy.

Though we didn't see eye-to-eye on many things, we agreed on what was best overall for his Battalion and our Brigade. I definitely trusted his combat and tactical decision making, and was very glad he was here. His take-charge attitude told me that we were starting to turn this thing around.

I ran through what was being done in my head . . .

Step 1: Lock down the perimeter. Montcalm and Stevenson were on top of that.

Step 2: Gather as much intel as possible. Major Warren was leading us here.

Step 3: Start a methodical search. We all had a part in this.

Major Warren had assumed the role of Commander on the ground. He received constant updates on the overall security of the perimeter and on the search for the enemy.

He found Air-Butler, back from the aid station, and sent him to find the two Kuwaiti interpreters that the Sergeant had brought into the Camp just a few hours earlier. The interpreters had been thoroughly vetted through the translator process and were approved to translate.

We realized that we knew very little more than the fact that they could speak English and that they were not Iraqi soldiers. They were our first suspects after we realized that there had been no change to our security or the camp with the exception of their arrival. We were beginning to realize that the grenade attacks were likely coming from the inside.

The interpreters were last seen with the Chaplain near the barriers outside the tents that were destroyed. When Air-Butler, Warren, and Hedrick caught up with the interpreters at the barriers, the men were surprised to see the interpreters standing there in the midst of all the chaos. They were not trying to evade or run.

The interpreters were neither helping to aid our wounded nor running to hide from our soldiers. They just stood there, in a daze, almost as if they were anxious to be found.

Explosions and gunfire had not been what they had signed up for, at least not while still in Kuwait at Camp Pennsylvania. When they arrived at the camp, they wore civilian clothes. Even now, in their Army-issued DCUs, they stood out.

"Gentlemen, we need to move you out of this area to a more secure area away from this location," Warren said to the two Kuwaitis.

"I need you to secure these two individuals," he said, turning to Smitty and another soldier standing nearby.

The interpreters, who just two and a half hours earlier were treated like part of the Coalition Force that they were, knew immediately that the situation had dramatically changed.

At first glance, Smitty along with most of the rest of us, had no idea that they were interpreters. However, Hedrick made it clear that these men were our interpreters, and directed that they not be mistreated.

The group walked to the right side of the tents with the interpreters holding their hands high in the air until told to stop and get on their knees.

"Do you understand English?" Warren asked the Kuwaitis.

They nodded in the affirmative.

Smitty and her counterpart had their M4 rifles pointed squarely at the back of the interpreters' heads. Their hands were placed behind their heads with fingers interlocked. They looked as if they thought that they were going to be executed.

"Do you understand that people think that you did this tonight?" Warren asked them.

Again, they both nodded, "Yes."

"A thousand apologies in the morning if this is a mistake," Hedrick said, mindful of the Brigade's directive to treat everyone with respect. "If anything happens tonight that gives you the impression that we don't respect you, again, a thousand apologies."

With that said, the male guard did a complete search of the interpreters' clothing and body. While Smitty dared them to move a muscle, the guard aggressively pat down every area, but he found nothing.

Flex handcuffs were placed on them, and they were told to stand up, first one and then the other. With rifles pointed at their backs, they were escorted in the vicinity of the TOC to be secured and questioned further.

The Brigade Combat Team's Military Intelligence Company interrogators were brought to the Command Center. They interrogated the two Kuwaitis to see if they were involved or had any knowledge of someone else who may have been.

Warren ordered that the interpreters' equipment be checked for any signs that they might be responsible for the night's horror.

While the guards kept their watchful eye on the two men, another soldier removed their equipment from Tent #2 and brought it outside. They were concerned that explosives could still be in their belongings.

Captain Butera was chosen to test the equipment. He attached a long piece of 550 cord to the equipment to check if it was rigged to somehow explode.

As the Interpreters looked on, he carefully moved the equipment to a safe distance from the rest of the troops. He walked in the opposite direction, as far away as the cord would allow. Then he yanked hard in an attempt to detonate the contents.

Nothing happened.

The interpreters professed to being victims, and appeared as clueless as the rest of us. During the whole 10-minute ordeal, they were more petrified than any of us, and undoubtedly surprised that our camp had been attacked.

You could see it in their face; they were shaking scared. These were not the eyes of cold-blooded killers.

Before this moment, knowing their arrival was the only change of the night made me sure it was them, and Warren agreed. We were both wrong.

But if not these men, then who?

* * *

Colonel Hodges was in the Command Center talking to Major General David Petraeus on the handset. Hodges was updating the General on everything, including the outcome of the interrogation of the two Kuwaiti interpreters.

The Commanding General was especially interested in the interpreters' story, and wanted more details.

The handset was passed to Hedrick, who had the most interaction with them. He explained the situation and said he did not believe they committed the attack.

As I watched our leaders update the General, my focus returned to the mystery of the enemy.

How did they get in? How did they create all of this devastation and then disappear, just like that? We were too good of a unit to be attacked and to let them get away. Though attacked while we slept, we were better than this, I thought to myself.

With the alert of the sirens and the SCUD attack, I was sure that it was all a part of a coordinated attack. At the same time, I just had not seen the evidence on the ground. The enemy couldn't have been that good!

More than 4,500 soldiers resided at this Camp, and no one had seen anyone who looked like the enemy. It felt like a crime that had happened in plain view, but left no witnesses on the worst streets in the country, where everyone is right there and no one is talking.

I was extremely frustrated that the enemy was still at large in the cold, dark desert.

* * *

The TOC was livelier now, full of bodies busily going about trying to find a lead in this lurid crime. This time, the buzz seemed different than before. As I approached the main command desk, the Colonel stepped in front of me, cutting me off abruptly to gain my attention.

"I got accountability from all of the units and everyone is accounted for except one," Hodges said with his eyes widening. "There's one soldier missing from Second Battalion. He's with the 326th Engineers. His name is Sergeant Akbar."

The Colonel's words meant absolutely nothing to me at first. I didn't realize he was trying to tell me this young soldier was trying to kill us. I thought Hodges was saying Sergeant Hasan Akbar may have fallen into the hands of the enemy, taken hostage, or maybe he was dead in the desert.

"Their Second Battalion ammunition had been broken into and there are fragmentary and incendiary grenades missing, along with 5.56mm ammunition," Hodges said. "Lieutenant Colonel Chris Hughes has every reason to believe that he (Akbar) did it and is our most likely suspect."

I paused in utter disbelief. My jaw wide open, I stared into a corner of the TOC, not fully knowing what exactly to say or how to say it. I wanted to ask him to repeat what he had just said, even though it was crystal clear. I had to let it register.

We were about to start a camp-wide search, looking for someone who boarded the plane with us from Fort Campbell, KY. We had met the enemy . . . and the enemy was one of us.

CHAPTER 7
Capture

We were facing the most improbable of adversaries, one of our own—an Embedded Enemy. The enemy looked like us. He dressed like us. He spoke like us. He had the ultimate camouflage.

I understood the sensitivity of this new intelligence. I needed to proceed with caution. I had to relay this horrifying update to my fellow soldiers without causing a panic. For one of the few times in my career, I could not even respond to Colonel Hodges with the traditional Army confirmation—"Hooah!"

If in fact Sergeant Akbar had committed this unfathomable crime, we wanted to catch him, and we wanted to catch him . . . now!

I was haunted by the thought that he could continue shooting at us, throwing grenades for the rest of the night, and never be suspected. I turned and briskly walked away from the Colonel to go out and alert the senior leadership that we had an Embedded Enemy.

Sergeant Akbar was the guy we wanted. He would be hard to find with most of the camp dark, which was compounded by the fact that he wore the same desert camouflage uniform as the rest of us.

I felt so angry that the person who had done this was a man who had taken the same oath of enlistment to defend the Constitution of the United States of America, against all enemies foreign and domestic. Tonight he treated us as the enemy. It was our turn to return the favor.

* * *

As I joined the search for Akbar, my mind filled with all of the possible scenarios of when and how I might have crossed paths with him that night. Did I pass him wearing my night-vision gear after leaving the Command Center? Was he one of the soldiers that I directed to a firing position along the Jersey barrier-lined perimeter.

I would not have thought to take any action toward him, unless his weapon was pointed directly at me or he was taking shots in my direction. Therefore, he could have just walked right up to me in that uniform, and shot me right in the face.

I shuddered at the idea.

As I made my way through the Command Center tent flaps, I deliberated as to how I was going to tell the soldiers, and considered which soldiers I should tell. I struggled with how exactly to word the alert so that I did not instigate a rampage of friendly fire with everyone thinking that they were shooting Akbar.

We wanted everyone to know so that we could increase our chances of catching the perpetrator faster. At the same time, to prevent a panic, we knew not everyone should know. Telling them to look for "a black guy in DCUs" would be a sure way to start such a panic.

The first person I saw when exiting the tent was Air-Butler. I pulled him to the side and whispered low, "We're looking for a guy named Akbar. He's one of our own. He has the same uniform on as we have on, DCUs. He was guarding the ammo and took some grenades and ammo. Be careful who you tell that to."

"Roger, Sergeant Major," Air-Butler replied.

Next, I searched for Burns, Montcalm, and Stevenson. These guys, like Air-Butler, were warfighters who knew how to handle information like this. They would know whom to tell and what to do. I found the First Sergeant in the open space that separated the TOC and tent row.

"First Sergeant, you're not going to believe this shit," I said to Stevenson. "It's a dude named Akbar. He's one of us."

"You bullshittin'," the First Sergeant said. "Are you serious?"

"Yep," I confirmed. "He took grenades and ammo from their Class V (supply cache)."

"I've seen him before," Stevenson said, recalling the name. "I don't know him, but I've seen him."

"He has on DCUs so be careful," I warned. "And watch who you tell. We don't want this spreading and soldiers shooting all over the damn place."

"Roger," he replied.

I went to the area where I last saw Montcalm. His men were still in the security posture, securing the right and rear sides of the perimeter. I was extremely thankful that they were there. I told Montcalm the news.

"I just saw him; he was on guard," he said, adding that he last saw him no more than two hours earlier.

"Well, we think that he did it. Grenades and ammo are missing and so is he," I replied.

Montcalm acknowledged that he understood.

The hunt for Sergeant Hasan Akbar was now on.

The senior NCOs in the operations headquarters now all knew what we were up against. They knew exactly who we were looking for, and what they needed to do—find Akbar.

It had been roughly 45 minutes since a shot was last fired or an explosion had happened. We wondered both what started the rampage and what stopped it. Had Akbar escaped, defected, or committed suicide to avoid detection and capture?

We were not even sure he had committed the crime. At this point, we had already accused two innocent people; we did not want to make the same mistake again.

While the sirens continued to blare as per SOP, SPC Jeanette Smith eventually took security in a dark, 12-foot long bunker where she found several soldiers already gathered. She immediately assumed the role of her day job, administrative specialist, by accounting for everyone and taking names. Just as everyone was accounted for, a new soldier arrived, and upon entry, threw some type of bag into the bunker that no one could identify. Smitty asked him his name and he did not respond. She asked again and still there was no response. It was Akbar and the bag contained grenades.

* * *

Major Warren was securing the perimeter and supervising the interrogation of the interpreters when the rest of us heard about Akbar. He returned to the TOC tent to update Colonel Hodges on the interrogation when the Colonel broke the news.

"No Slack's accountability report had one guy unaccounted for, a Sergeant Akbar," Hodges said. "And there are some ammunition and grenades missing, from their area."

Warren had never heard that name before. His face said it all: Everything tonight was completely unexpected.

He left the main Command Center and stood in front of the tent's vestibule, revisiting the things he had seen in just a few short hours. One of his soldiers, a Captain, was severely injured and he didn't have an update on his status; several explosions left soldiers on guard, tense, and very nervous; the threat of fratricide filled the air; and now he was told that one of our own might be responsible.

Feeling secure about the security of the perimeter, fratricide was now Warren's biggest concern, particularly in light of the new information. He decided to walk back toward the area where the tents lay smoldering. He wanted to talk to the senior NCOs about how to share this new information. He would need their help to disseminate it down through their informal chain of command as calmly as possible.

As he walked into the night, Warren noticed a lone bunker, about 30 meters in front of him and to his right, just outside of the perimeter. From where he stood, he could not see if anyone was in the bunker, so he went to check. As he began to walk in that direction, he came to the realization that Akbar could still be in the area. The thought of it instantly heightened his sense of alert.

As Warren got halfway to the bunker, he greeted the occupants the same way he had all night, "Hey, who do we got out here?"

The first response he heard was a voice saying, "Sergeant Akbar." He got a little closer to the bunker with his pistol still in his hand, when he thought better of it. He decided that the best thing to do was to holster his 9mm so that he would not appear to be a threat.

As he slid the weapon in the holster, he tried to lower his body tension and get his fear under control. His adrenaline had been up and down all night.

As his body went on full alert, Warren walked slowly toward Akbar's voice. He had only heard the name once before—just now when the Colonel told him about the Embedded Enemy. Since this was only the second time he had ever heard Akbar's name, he wasn't even sure if he had heard it correctly. He worked hard to maintain his composure as he approached the Sergeant.

Akbar seemed to be oblivious to the fact that people were looking for him. He had blended in with the soldiers in their same security posture. How odd to be protecting himself from . . . himself.

This wasn't Warren's first time in a life-threatening situation. In the early 1990s, a soldier posing as a highly decorated combat veteran shot his First Sergeant, and then turned the weapon on himself. All of the ifs of that experience still haunted Warren. He wished he had done more back then to save his First Sergeant.

This was his second chance. Warren stayed mindful that being tense and showing aggression would likely trigger Akbar into his firing at our soldiers again, starting with Warren, who was closest to Akbar's crosshairs.

Warren finally walked close enough to look directly into Akbar's eyes. His eyes searched Akbar's helmet for the embroidery on his helmet band. It read A–K–B–A–R.

He was trying not to shake, keeping himself as calm as possible. He asked the other soldier who was visible in the bunker with Akbar to also identify himself. He didn't want to give away that Akbar was the person he wanted.

As the other soldier spoke, Warren walked closer, trying to keep the situation calm, so that he could position himself behind Akbar. The carnage that Warren had seen in the tents and the gore and bloodshed of the crime that Akbar committed quickly flashed through the Major's head. He knew that he was face-to-face with a murderer.

Was he really trained for this? Police officers regularly attend combatives training. But Warren had been an Infantryman, an Infantry Lieutenant, and now an Intelligence Officer. His last hand-to-hand combat training was long, long ago. His last fistfight was even further in the past. To boot, he had lost weight in the desert, making his already small frame even less menacing. He wasn't sure that he was in a position to take on a man that had at least 35 pounds on him.

Akbar was in an aiming position, kneeling on his right knee, leaning on his right shoulder, up against the inside of the bunker. His weapon pointed out in the direction of the desert.

Warren had not thought about what he would actually do until he was already moving behind Akbar. Luckily, his training kicked in. He instinctively turned and used the Infantry ambush tactic. With the element of surprise, he grabbed Akbar by the shoulders and attempted to push him forward to the ground.

Akbar was in that stable kneeling position, which thwarted Warren's full momentum. He did, however, have enough momentum to dislodge Akbar's weapon, but the bunker helped Akbar to stay upright. As Warren pushed, Akbar resisted. Warren realized that he didn't have enough weight to push Akbar down.

He knew that he had to establish a better position of power, so he used his chest, thrusting it hard into Akbar's back. At the same time, he reached around with his left hand to grab the front of Akbar's helmet. Warren continued to push forward and simultaneously pull the helmet hard enough to bring Akbar down face first to the ground.

The huge shift of weight left Warren way off balance, losing a bit of his power base. That power base was crucial if Warren was going to win this grappling match. He was able to plant his foot on the upper portion of Akbar's back, near his neck.

Even still he was a bit off balance, holding himself up by the Jersey barrier just outside the bunker. Warren slid his foot back a little from Akbar's neck and replaced it with his left hand in between the shoulder blades. Warren dropped his left knee down, allowing it to apply pressure in the small of Akbar's back. Warren finally felt on top.

The wrestling match was over.

Warren drew his weapon and pointed it directly between Akbar's shoulders. Warren told Akbar to spread eagle with his arms pushed out just slightly above his shoulders and his legs opened wide.

Warren then ordered Akbar to use his toes to push himself out and away from the bunker. When Akbar had moved three to four feet, and the majority of his body was away from the bunker, Warren re-aimed his 9mm and said, "Don't you f*****g move!"

Now that the struggle with Akbar was over, Warren realized that the soldier behind him who had just witnessed the whole incident—and never lifted a finger to help—might shoot him, thinking that Warren had unjustifiably attacked Akbar.

"I'm Major Warren," he barked to the soldier. "I need you to get out of the bunker and guard him."

The soldier moved around to the left of the prisoner, a few feet away and settled into a vigilant overwatch position with his weapon pointed directly at Akbar.

Warren now felt safe to stand up and move away from Akbar. He re-holstered his weapon and moved around to Akbar's right. He faced the prisoner and knelt down on all fours, two feet away from Akbar's face. Warren wanted Akbar to be able to see and hear him clearly.

"Did you do this?" Major Warren yelled at Akbar. "Did you bomb the tents?"

"YES!" Akbar said. He was somber and unapologetic. Warren said Akbar seemed relieved that it was over.

* * *

While Akbar's confession was a big step toward closing this horrible chapter in our lives, it was only the first step. Now we had to deescalate the situation, clean up the mess, and make this man pay for his crimes.

"Do not move," Warren said to Akbar through gritted teeth. "If you move, he will shoot you in the head."

Warren looked up to see Burns and Air-Butler walking toward them.

The earlier teamwork of Burns and Stevenson provided more light to the camp; Burns, by restoring power to the generator lights in the tent area, and Stevenson, by suggesting the use of vehicle headlights to aid in the search for the enemy, provided a visibility they would not have otherwise had. Unfortunately, the headlights failed to reach the bunker housing Warren and Akbar, so they were in the shadows as the two Sergeants approached.

"That's him; that's Akbar," Burns declared as he saw Warren with his knee in Akbar's back and the other soldier with his weapon drawn. Warren summoned Burns and Air-Butler over to guard and search Akbar, thereby relieving the soldier. He put the two men in charge of the scene. Akbar was not going to slip through their fingers now.

The headlights caught my attention, so I headed over to find out what was going on. That is when I saw him—his face was still in the sand with his head turned to one side.

Warren holstered his firearm since Air-Butler had taken over security. He had his World War II M14 rifle pointed squarely at Akbar's back.

"If you make one move, I will take that to mean resistance and I will shoot you," Air-Butler said. "Do you understand?"

"Yes," Akbar replied.

Once there was a clear understanding of life or death, Burns began conducting a search of Akbar's body for any other weapons. Warren had already taken Akbar's M4.

With Akbar on his belly, I watched Burns perform his search by the numbers. I also had an eye on Air-Butler, as I believed he would shoot Akbar if he sneezed the wrong way.

Burns told Air-Butler, "Clear," which meant that he hadn't found anything on his backside from head to toe. He then reached for his plastic flex-cuffs and affixed them to Akbar's wrists. I could feel the pressure that Air-Butler was applying with that barrel in Akbar's back. I said nothing.

* * *

CBS's news crew, Strassmann and Lee, had found their way to the vicinity of the Command Center where Hodges gave Strassmann the news.

"We think that it was one of our own who did this," Hodges said.

"What are you talking about?" Strassmann replied.

"It's an American," Hodges said, looking the newsman in the eye.

The news crew quickly located Akbar. Burns was conducting the search when Lee started the camera. Akbar was still facedown in the desert sand.

Once he secured the flex-cuffs, Burns pulled Akbar to his knees and then stood him up. I was standing to the side of Burns when he stood Akbar up. The prisoner's DCU top rose up, pulling his brown T-shirt out of his pants.

That's when I saw a small knife dangle from a piece of 550 cord that was attached to one of the belt loops of his pants.

"Wait a minute," I said. "There's a knife."

It was a three-inch, hook-blade knife. Not a normal Army field knife. It looked like it might be used to gut a small animal.

It sure would have taken a nice chunk out of a human being as well.

I grabbed it, yanking as hard as I could, popping the belt loop from the pants. I stuck it in my pocket to keep my hands free, just in case I needed them for something else.

Aside from Akbar's confession, we would still need proof that he attacked us. Possibly from watching too much CSI on TV before we deployed, I thought we might be able to match the ammunition in his weapon with the ammunition that had been fired at Romaine and Seifert. Therefore, I redirected my focus to finding Akbar's weapon and then returning to the scene of the crime to find evidence linking the two.

The Army numbers its rounds of ammunition with a Department of Defense Ammunition Code, or DoDAC. When I returned earlier to the remnants of my tent after the outside generator lights were back on, I had seen a 5.56mm brass cartridge laying on the ground on the left, front side of the tent entrance. I knew at that time that it was evidence.

Now, I needed to find Akbar's weapon to see if it was a match. If he were the shooter, his weapon would still have the fresh smell of gunshot residue, known as GSR. It should be the only weapon that had been fired that night, so there would be no confusing it as the murder weapon.

"Air-Butler, where's his weapon?" I asked.

"Over here Sergeant Major," Air-Butler said as he gestured with his head, not taking his eyes off of Akbar. Butler's weapon was still squarely attached to Akbar's back with his trigger finger itching.

I walked over and secured Akbar's rifle. It was a standard-issue Army M4 rifle with a 40mm grenade launcher attached to create an M203.

First, I made sure that the safety was on to prevent a negligent discharge. That was when I noticed that the magazine was still in the weapon and a round was chambered. Under normal circumstances, I would have removed the magazine, extracted the round in the chamber, and cleared the weapon.

But this time, things were very different. I wanted the weapon in the state that Akbar had left it. It would make for an immediate match of the DoDACs if it was the murder weapon. The expended cartridges on the ground would match the rounds that were in the magazine.

To check my theory and maintain the evidence, I held the rifle—the best potential link so far between Akbar and the shootings—out in front of me, grasping the hand guard and the barrel at the front sight post. I turned it horizontal to the ground, with the barrel pointing in a safe direction in the desert, while moving it close to my nose.

I took a nice long inhale as if it were a chocolate chip cookie right out of the oven. The aroma of the fresh GSR rushed up my nose and stopped in my throat. It was clear confirmation that this weapon had been fired within the hour, two tops. Plus that same scent would be on his hands, unless he fired wearing gloves.

"Do you want the grenades too Sergeant Major?" Air-Butler asked, watching me gather up Akbar's other weapons.

"What grenades?" I replied.

"Akbar had some grenades in his protective mask carrier, I put them in the bunker," he said.

When Air-Butler learned that Akbar was believed to have grenades with him, Air-Butler asked Akbar if he had any more on his person. Akbar told him that more grenades were in his protective mask carrier, which was the same bag he tossed in the bunker moments earlier near Smitty and her comrades.

Air-Butler picked up the carrier, feeling the full weight of more grenades, each weighing in at 14 ounces. Knowing Akbar was an engineer, Air-Butler did not open the carrier to double check, fearing that it could be booby-trapped. Instead, Air-Butler took the carrier to the closest safe place, the same SCUD bunker where Akbar was apprehended. The bunker would protect everyone if the grenades were detonated.

"I'll take a look at them, but I do not want them," I said. "Show them to me."

Burns took over the duties of security guard so Air-Butler could take me to the grenade-packed carrier. With Akbar now sitting on the ground with his legs crossed, Burns pointed his weapon directly at Akbar's head.

Air-Butler escorted me to the bunker, reached in, and pulled out the protective mask carrier.

"I didn't open it," he said. "I thought that it could be booby-trapped."

I hesitated for a second, knowing that Akbar was an engineer. However, I quickly ruled it out thinking that Akbar clearly wanted routine and easy access so he could use all of them in the attack. Something clearly stopped his rampage.

I opened up the carrier and saw the unused grenades inside. He had at least one incendiary and one fragmentary grenade left. One starts fires and the other will blow a person into very small pieces. Neither option was good. I gave the carrier back to Air-Butler.

"Just leave them in here," I said. "This is a good place for them. Find someone to guard them."

We now were growing a good case against our suspect. We had a cache of Akbar's weapons, the smell of GSR on the weapon, and a magazine with rounds we might be able to match to the bullet casings at the scene.

Carrying Akbar's M203, I went to my tent to look in the vicinity where I had seen the expended brass casing earlier that evening. Luckily, I walked right to it. I could feel my heart race, but I had to think calmly; I had to decide how to best preserve the evidence.

The area was still full of confusion with people moving all over the place. I looked for a good Noncommissioned Officer whom I could trust to guard the weapon and the brass casing until I relieved them.

Staff Sergeant Timothy Gray, our recruitment NCO, received the honors. I had trusted this loyal career soldier implicitly since our days at Fort Campbell where he did an outstanding job keeping talented soldiers in the Army. His pleasant, no-nonsense demeanor coupled with his commitment to the Army made him the perfect guy to guard this vital evidence.

"Sergeant, I want you to guard this weapon and this brass casing until I relieve you," I said. "Only I can relieve you, no one else. And don't let anyone come near it. Make them walk all the way around the tent if they have to. Do you understand?"

"Yes, Sergeant Major," he said.

I knew without a doubt that this rifle and the casing were solid, concrete evidence and should not be disturbed.

I left to grab my body armor and helmet from my tent. With the generators back on, I could see the devastation much more clearly. The night was not over, but at least I could now protect my body.

The smell, though dissipated from earlier, was still suffocating as I walked through the vestibule into the tent. I opened the flaps wide so that some light could enter. It was dismal. Holding the flaps with my left hand, I looked on the left, front side of the tent, where I had last put my gear. I got a visual, took a few steps, and walked straight to it. It had a dark and eerie feel.

The adrenaline flowing in my body following the capture of Akbar had my heart and mind racing. I felt no fear. But now, knowing what had happened just 90 minutes earlier and how close I had come to dying, I started to feel sick. I quickly grabbed my gear and got out of there.

The hard part was about to begin—proving Akbar did this, and why.

CHAPTER 8
Evidence

Sergeant Hasan Akbar's confession to Major Warren was emphatic enough to convince us that he was the attacker. But it would not be enough for a court martial.

Warren knew that a lot more had to be done, and it had to be done just right. Akbar was an American citizen who had rights, rights that needed to be explained to him.

"We have to do this right; we have to do this right," Warren repeated to himself as he considered all of the steps before him. He knew that the capture and battlefield confession would not be enough to keep Akbar behind bars.

The Major was hyper-vigilant about making sure he found the right person and the right place to administer Akbar's rights to him, and he knew that he was not the right person and this secluded bunker was not the right place.

Warren sent for Sergeant Eric Tanner, the Brigade's legal NCO. He was the perfect person to administer the rights and give the proper legal advice to guide him through this tangled mess.

"We have a soldier detained out by the bunker," Warren told Tanner as soon as he arrived on the scene. "We need to make sure that we read him his rights and do this correctly. We've got to do this right."

"This is a soldier. It is not a Kuwaiti interpreter. It is not an Iraqi enemy," he continued. "We need to make sure we do this correctly since we're dealing with an American soldier. I can't read him his rights as I was the one who apprehended him."

A Warrant Officer, who had been interrogating the interpreters, and Captain Williams, who had just stepped out of the TOC, joined the two men in their huddle. Both men happened to walk by about that time, so they became "volunteers" in the military sense.

Tanner pointed out that he, as the legal arm of the commander, could not read the rights nor question Akbar with the intent of using any information for his prosecution. He added that Williams was not eligible to recite Akbar's rights because, even though he was not in his tent at the time of the attack and escaped harm, he had been a target. The Warrant Officer was the only one in the huddle with no link to the attacks.

"You're in charge of reading him his rights," Warren said to the Warrant Officer. "Sergeant Tanner, you are there to provide legal expertise so that he does this correctly. Captain Williams, you are in charge of making sure that nobody hinders [the Warrant Officer's] ability to conduct this.

"Do you guys understand?"

They all nodded.

"Remember, we've got to make sure that we do this right, every step of the way," Warren told the men.

* * *

Sergeant Burns continued to guard Akbar as the senior military leadership worked out a plan for handling the prisoner. He was doing his best to keep his cool, but something bubbled up inside of him.

"Why? Why did you do this?" Burns yelled at Akbar.

Burns was so infuriated that he cut Akbar off as soon as he began to utter a sound.

"Shut up!" Burns yelled.

Akbar lowered his head, looking no more than a foot in front of where he was sitting. It was then that Burns noticed Akbar's right pant leg was starting to show blood. He must have suffered shrapnel wounds from one of the grenade explosions. We now had another potential issue on our hands.

About this time, I returned to the area where the prisoner was being detained—only about 100 feet from the bustling Command Center. I was furious. My mind was swirling with the realization that anyone, let alone this person—someone that was supposed to be a fellow soldier—had not only tried to kill me but also cremate me tonight.

I wanted revenge, not just for myself but also for all of our comrades who lay injured and dying. As I stomped back to see the detainee, a dozen revenge fantasies flew through my mind. They all played out by the time I arrived. I knew that two wrongs didn't make a right, as the saying goes. Nor did I want to be remembered the same way Akbar would, as a cold-blooded, ruthless killer. So I gathered my wits and joined the small group around the prisoner, and just observed.

Before we could make Akbar aware of his rights, Warren needed to find a better place to house him. He searched for a location that would protect and keep Akbar out of sight of the soldiers, away from the sleeping tents, but still within the perimeter of the headquarters area.

A good place would have been the logistics tent just outside the TOC, but the interpreters were already in there. We were still holding them under guard for their safety. We had mistaken them for the enemy once and didn't want to expose them to others who might do the same.

We were wary of drawing attention to people under guard by moving them around. So Warren chose an area out by the port-a-johns, just east of the bunker where Akbar had been captured. The lights from the vehicle that had been placed there earlier illuminated the area. It was here that Akbar was read his rights.

* * *

After nabbing Akbar from the bunker, Warren quickly briefed Colonel Hodges. The verbal rundown of the night's events was the first real opportunity Warren had to digest what had happened. It was his opportunity to exhale and get it all out.

I took the knife out of my pocket that I had confiscated earlier from Akbar and showed it to the Colonel, informing him that I had yanked it off of Akbar during the search. I also told him that I left the suspect's weapon near the expended cartridge with a guard. I hoped that we had all of the critical pieces of evidence to build a case against the suspect.

Hodges was on the phone with General Petraeus, giving him the last update regarding our suspicion that the attack was from one of our soldiers.

The look of total disbelief spread across the faces of everyone present in the Command Center as they heard about Akbar's capture. How could someone, especially a "so-called" soldier, fathom even the idea of taking the lives of his or her fellow soldiers?

I paced around the TOC, playing back the night's events in my head. By now it had been about two hours since the first smoking grenade rolled to my feet.

I overheard someone say that the Criminal Investigative Division (CID) was on their way to our location at the request of Division Headquarters. I paced back and forth in the TOC listening to the radios and the buzz created by the capture of Akbar. I could not just stand there waiting for answers like everyone else. So I headed once again to ask Akbar myself.

Just as I walked up to the illuminated area where Akbar was being held, I heard Burns ask him what we all wanted to ask him, "Why did you do this?"

There was a long pause. "You told me to shut up," he finally replied.

"Now you can talk," Burns said in much calmer voice. "Why did you do this?"

"You guys are coming into our countries, and you're going to rape our women and kill our children," Akbar said with a calm voice.

Burns and Air-Butler, who were guarding the suspect, both seemed to be holding their breath at the response.

I didn't move. I wasn't sure which word shocked me the most: "rape," "kill," or "our"!

I was pretty sure that no one in this command had the intention to rape an Iraqi woman or to kill an Iraqi child. I realized now how little I really knew about Akbar. I had never considered that he might be Iraqi or have any relatives in Iraq, Kuwait, or anywhere in the Middle East for that matter.

Two of my nephews are devout, practicing, active Muslims—one for 30 years and the other for about 15 years. I 100 percent support their religious beliefs and have never heard either one of them make the claims Akbar made that night.

As the temperature began to drop in the early morning hours, I saw a soldier wrap a poncho around Akbar. I couldn't make out who it was, and I didn't care to ascertain if it was the right thing to do. Though an hour or so before, Akbar was trying to kill the same soldier who was now making him comfortable.

Though no one removed it, onlookers began to whisper in disbelief that someone actually cared enough about Akbar to make the gesture. But that's the spirit of the American GI, to adhere to the Geneva Convention and take care of the captured enemy.

This was no ordinary enemy. This man had committed treason. I highly doubt few other countries' soldiers would have treated him so well.

* * *

Headlights of an SUV approached the TOC near where Akbar was being held. The doors swung open and two criminal investigators, called CID agents, stepped out. They reported inside the Command Center before quickly being escorted back out of the tent and to where Akbar was being held.

The CID agents placed hard, steely handcuffs on Akbar and removed the plastic flex-cuffs. CID assumed full control and security of the prisoner as Burns and Air-Butler stepped away.

Before CID could leave, Burns had another surprise for us.

"Sergeant Major, it was two people," he said, looking straight at me.

"What?" I asked.

"When Captain Seifert got shot, I saw the guy who shot him run one way, and I saw someone else run in a different direction," Burns said.

"Are you sure?"

"I'm positive."

"Shhhit," I said.

I had known Burns for 14 years and trusted him wholeheartedly. I had no reason to doubt his word.

My mind raced through the 130 Headquarters personnel, and I quickly ruled them all out. But this left more than 4,000 more people to consider.

Just as we were contemplating whom the "second man" could be, a soldier approached the Brigade area from the left of where we were standing. He was about 75 yards away, and the lights from the generator had him fully illuminated. While he did not appear to be a threat, we were not in the mood to take chances.

"Halt!" Burns yelled out. "Who are you?"

His nametag wasn't visible from that distance. He mumbled his name.

"Drop your weapon and get on your knees!" Burns ordered.

The unidentified man bent over slowly and placed his weapon on the ground.

"Put your hands on your head," Burns said. "Why are you here?'

"I got lost," the soldier replied with a slight smile.

He definitely chose the wrong night to get lost. After a short pause, he was told to pick up his weapon and go back to his unit. I wondered how many times we were going to challenge our soldiers here at Camp Pennsylvania.

* * *

The early morning of March 23 had entered with a boom. The worst seemed over, but the explosions were really just the beginning.

When Colonel Hodges was on the phone with Division, he was informed by the Public Affairs Officer that someone assigned to our unit had been on the phone to the States.

It turned out to be Lacey, who by now thought he'd better get back to being a journalist and called Time Magazine on his satellite phone. They were very excited to hear from him and inserted the call into television and radio shows for 15-20 minutes.

Division advised Colonel Hodges to get the reporter under control. All of the facts were not in, so we did not want the journalist reporting as if they were. We were particularly concerned that it would be reported that Akbar was Muslim. We were not sure he was, despite his confession and explanation for the crime. We wanted it to be confirmed before we released this volatile information.

The Colonel gathered the media who were huddled around the TOC, growing restlessly eager for more details.

"We have a situation here that is still not secure," Hodges told the reporters. "We have a lot of injured soldiers, and I want you to use your judgment as fellow human beings as to what that information will mean for families back home."

The reporters were under pressure to bring the action of the front lines into the livings rooms of hometown America as best as they could. This was their first test, and it was a complex test not covered in training.

They were patient, professional, and cooperative, and they respected our security concerns. They were willing to work with us and wait until we could get the facts. After first directing Lacey to shut up and get off the air, or be sent home, the Division Public Affairs Officer called back and said that Lacey could be on the air for as long as he needed, seeing as the President of the United States had just quoted him on TV. Although, he was still not permitted to mention specific details referencing the casualties.

Once the facts were confirmed, Colonel Hodges called the media together again. Our CBS crew and Lacey had now been joined by onlooker soldiers who wanted the latest updates.

Hodges stood in front of everyone with his pant legs stained in blood and his right arm heavily bandaged in a sling. He looked a mess and was a telling the story of this horrific night.

The Commander faced the camera crew with these terrible injuries, all incurred from one of his very own soldiers. The lights were on and the camera rolled as the Colonel stood with his back to the TOC. He calmly and succinctly gave them his account of what had happened and what led to Akbar's capture.

Within a few minutes, the Colonel parted the reporters and walked toward me. I had been standing a few feet away watching the interview. In a low voice that no one else could hear, Hodges told me that the reporters wanted to interview me, and asked if I would be willing. I agreed and returned to the media as the Colonel stepped back.

The chaotic atmosphere outside the TOC made for great background noise for the viewers so they could understand the dramatic scene, but the sound was difficult for the news organizations to edit out. The lights were on, but it still was not enough light or quiet for the camera crews. So the camera crew took over the TOC, people were asked to be quiet, radios were turned off, and lighting was adjusted.

Quickly thinking of the night's events, playing them back in my head from the terrible start, made the moisture in my mouth disappear. My throat was tight and adrenaline was pumping through my veins. I took a deep breath, bringing the air through my nose, and exhaled as smoothly as I could through my mouth.

My only prep for the interview was Strassmann saying all he wanted was a recap of the night's events with a few follow-up questions. Neither the lights nor the camera stuck in my face bothered me; it was the thought of whom the enemy had turned out to be that made me sick.

I barely had time to chug down some water before the questions started. In seconds, the lights were on and the cameras were rolling, and Strassmann was announcing his opening remarks. There I was—live—facing the world with the vivid news of this shocking, insane crime. I completely ignored everything and everybody in the room except Strassmann's questions. It was over before I realized I was talking.

They immediately dispersed to make the necessary editing adjustments and to get the footage on air. I found a chair and sat down. It was the first time that night that I had actually taken a moment to catch my breath.

* * *

With the news crews gone and the sun coming up, I had one more thing to do before I could head to breakfast to find something to pump up my blood sugar. I had been awake well over 24 hours.

So I tracked down one of the CID agents in the vicinity of the TOC to recount my story for the record, even though I had yet to make it official in a sworn statement.

I talked about how a grenade had been rolled into my tent just as Tiger was teeing off. I thought that it was a fragmentary grenade, manufactured from "the land of not quite right," so it sparked first before it exploded. Then I, upon seeing the sparks, ran to the back of the tent to awake the Colonel.

I tried to cover as much detail as I could, telling the story at a pace that only a dictation expert could follow. It was in their hands to peel back the onion, going step-by-step, gathering as much information as they could to make a future case for the government.

Hodges met me as I exited the tent after wrapping up with CID. He was still soaked in blood and refused medical help.

Knowing that arguing with him would do no good, we changed the subject and started talking about the next steps we needed to take.

We decided to start by gathering all of the walking wounded. We wanted to put together a convoy and take them all to the hospital for treatment. By now, the shrapnel fragments in their bodies were moving around, causing pain and possibly aggravating their injuries.

Though they had all functioned superbly all night, through the pain as first responders and guardians, it surely was not good for them in the long run.

We also needed to check on all of our soldiers who were medically evacuated, as well as those who were not. We knew that we likely had several injured soldiers who had suffered life-threatening injuries, but just did not know it yet.

We now had the sun on our side, and would soon get a much better view of what had just hit us.

* * *

Mark Strassmann's report from Kuwait, 23 March 2003:

Mark Strassmann began:

"Bedlam and possible betrayal jolted this camp awake overnight in Kuwait. In seconds, four grenades were tossed into three separate tents, where soldiers, mostly Officers of the First Brigade, 101st Airborne Division, were sleeping. In the tent of Colonel Ben Hodges, this camp's Commander, his Command Sergeant Major, Bart Womack, suddenly noticed sparks on their tent's floor."

Command Sergeant Major Bart Womack reported:

"I ran to the back of the tent, the Commander was back there asleep—I ran to the back of the tent to get him up and to simultaneously, to kind of, get him down away from the explosion.

"That grenade never exploded, but another one in his tent, and in two more, did, in tents that were directly behind mine. I heard two powerful booms, then screaming. When confused soldiers inside those tents ran outside, at least one of them was shot, investigators believe by the same attacker. Just as startling, the search quickly focused on a U.S. soldier, a Sergeant Engineer, living on this camp. He was found hiding in a bunker, wounded."

Colonel Ben Hodges reported:

"He became a suspect when, of course, after this all happened, we tried to get accountability of everybody. And we noticed that fragmentary hand grenades were missing, and that this Sergeant was unaccounted for.

"Five grenades, three fragmentary, and one incendiary were tossed into tents, and a fourth found inside the suspect's protective mask carrier. No motive was [given]. And then the unthinkable got even worse. Suddenly overhead, there was a flash in the sky. A U.S. Patriot missile had struck what was thought to be an Iraqi SCUD missile. But instead it apparently downed a British Tornado Fighter Jet returning from a mission. Both its crew are missing, on a night when tragedy came calling on the coalition in the desert not once, but twice."

For CBS Sunday Morning, this is Mark Strassmann, in Kuwait.

CHAPTER 9
The Fallout

With the sun lighting our way, we were able to identify five officers, including the chaplain, and one female private who needed medical attention.

We corralled the Command's drivers and gave them a warning order to get the vehicles ready. We were going to the hospital.

Everyone grabbed their gear—armored vest, Kevlar helmet, and weapon. I went into the TOC and grabbed another M4 rifle, having returned the first one to its rightful owner. My 9mm pistol was still empty. I had never found the time to go back and load rounds in its magazine.

My tent still had no interior lights due to the blast, but the sun was almost straight above and leaked through the tent walls that were now filled with holes from shrapnel. I was sure plenty of light was spilling in, but I was not sure that I was ready to go back and view the devastation.

I walked slowly toward the area of my tent, stopping at the pallets that led to its vestibule. Before heading off with the wounded, I wanted to check on Gray, the guard I had trusted with Akbar's weapon and the brass DODAC cartridge that we expected would connect the weapon to the crime.

Just as I had hoped and expected, Gray was still standing in the same spot just outside my tent, the same spot that I had left him hours ago in the dark.

"You're doing a good job, Ranger," I said. "Hang in there. Have someone bring you a chair so you can sit down."

"Do you know how much longer I'll be here, Sergeant Major?" Gray asked.

"No, but don't you move," I replied.

"Can I go to breakfast?" he asked with a straight back and strong voice.

"You can have someone bring you a to-go plate, or eat an MRE," I said. "But don't you move."

"Roger, Sergeant Major," he said as his back and voice relaxed.

Lacey received a stern reminder about his role with the unit—as a journalist and not a soldier. Shortly after a Sergeant walked by with his friends and said, "This is the guy who was playing soldier and hero last night." "Are you really a Colonel?" "Yes, Lieutenant Colonel, and shut up about anything I did. It might get me thrown out of country and sent back home," Lacey warned out of concern that his tour as a war journalist was coming to an abrupt end.

All of the injured rallied near the three Hummers and got a headcount of the personnel that would be leaving the camp for the nearest field hospital. We needed to report those numbers and names to the Command Center so we could begin to bring back a little order to this chaos.

I told Hodges that we counted him among those headed to the hospital ASAP. He stubbornly assured me that he was okay. He said his arm was just a little sore, indicating that was the end of the discussion.

Hodges, who was Camp Commander, then turned to LTC Hughes and told him to "hold down the Fort," thereby verbally appointing Hughes Command Authority until Hodges returned from getting his Soldiers their much-needed medical attention.

We loaded the trucks with our wounded and headed toward the Camp Pennsylvania gate, then on to the field hospital in Camp Udari just three miles away. It was a long, slow, quiet seven-minute ride.

What do you say when someone you trusted to have your back shoots you in it?

We approached the exit where the traditional military S-shaped path had been erected to slow vehicles down. As our Hummers approached, I could feel the guards' eyes bearing down on us.

The guards knew that tents in the Headquarters Company had been attacked but were not sure who was hurt or what the status was of the leaders. They were clearly relieved when they saw "COL Hodges" and "CSM Womack" written on the windshields of the two Hummers headed toward them. As each of our Hummers approached, the guards could see it really was us—alive and well.

The dust from the Colonel's vehicle in the lead left a big cloud over ours. We throttled back our speed to clear our visibility.

I raised my hand just above the flat dashboard and gave the guards a hand wave as I uttered the traditional Army, "Hooah!" I could feel the emotion welling up as I looked into their faces. I was very proud of them.

"We're on our way to the hospital," I said.

"Roger, Sergeant Major," the guard replied sporting a stern look and standing at his best position of "Parade Rest."

* * *

It was a short, bumpy trip that left us all covered in desert dust. Camp Udari, which housed the nearest field hospital, was also the home of the Division's Aviation Brigades and our Combat Team's two Aviation Battalions—3-101 and 5-101. On this trip, we did not have time to stop, check on them, and give them an update. They had no doubt heard the news of the attack over the radio and would have to get their updates the same way.

While I knew Camp Pennsylvania like the back of my hand, Camp Udari was a whole different ballgame. I was not clear on the exact location of the hospital in the Camp, so I throttled back on my navigational duties and let Allen take us there while I watched the helicopters on flight line.

The tent complex that made up the hospital looked like our own TOC pad but with a lot more tents. When we finally saw the sign announcing "86th Combat Support Hospital (CSH)," we parked in the designated parking area and climbed out of the trucks.

The first person of our group to enter asked the guard on duty for directions to the emergency area, and the rest of us followed like ducks in a row.

The hospital was a maze of tents and aboveground, tarp-covered tunnels that led to more tents. Each tent contained a different section of the hospital. The hospital seemed to have more corridors than the Pentagon. The place was huge and you could easily become disoriented.

Some tents were filled with beds and some with supplies. If it were Hollywood, you would have thought that you were inside a tent on an old episode of M*A*S*H.

After feeling like a rat in a maze, we finally made it to the emergency area that temporarily held our medevac'd soldiers. These were our most seriously injured, and two of the men taken out on the first bird—Holden and Stone.

Hodges, myself and some of the wounded who had just caravanned from the blast site gathered around a staffer who gave his best analysis of who was in what stage in the medical process and the status of their condition. He knew that Major Stone was in very bad shape and was currently in surgery. Based on his injuries, Stone had done well to make it to the hospital alive. Captain Holden was also in surgery and in only slightly better shape.

In the cold of the operating room, Holden had emerged from anesthesia just before they wheeled him out of surgery. He went under knowing he might lose his leg and dangling foot. He asked the doctors if it was still there, and they assured him it was.

Holden, still groggy from the anesthesia, looked down at his leg and told the doctors he could not see his leg.

"If you guys are lying, I'm gonna come back and kill all you sons of bitches," he said, then he busted out laughing.

The doctors propped his leg up on a pillow so he could see his leg better, then unwrapped the bandages to expose his toes.

"Okay, you guys are all safe now," Holden said after taking a few minutes to focus on his toes.

Returning to earth after his medically induced high, Holden had a visit in the field hospital from Major General Petraeus. Despite providing a few words of encouragement to Holden, the lead-from-front Company Commander felt the need to apologize to the General for sustaining an injury. Petraeus told Holden that it was not necessary to apologize, and to focus on his recovery.

We were glad Holden was in good spirits in spite of his injuries. Not wanting to hinder his recovery, we thought it was best to wait before we gave him any bad news. For now, he was completely unaware that the enemy was one of our own.

Shortly after arriving at the field hospital with our Hummers full of wounded, Hodges and I were officially informed that Captain Seifert had died of the complications from the gunshot to his back. We had been warned that it was a possibility before we left that morning, but we still held out a glimmer of hope.

When you lose a soldier as a leader, the loss has an affect on you that is impossible to explain. You feel that you let them down in some way, no matter what the circumstance.

With all of the visiting and reassuring done, it was time to get our walking wounded treated. All of the Soldiers we brought in our Hummers had small pieces of shrapnel lodged in their bodies. The Colonel, who had seemingly shed a lot of blood, ended up having only two pieces of shrapnel removed from his forearm. I was sure he was injured a lot worse given all of the blood on his uniform. But Colonel Hodges walked out of the hospital with just two Band-Aids on his arm.

As we left the hospital, we reassured everyone that they would be okay, and that we would see them soon, back in the fight, stronger than ever. The injured we left behind would fight hard to recover and rejoin the unit. It would take a miracle to see most of them again in Iraq before we redeployed.

* * *

As the bulk of our wounded were treated in the nearby CSH at Camp Udari, Seifert, Wisher, Romaine, and Armosolo were in the field hospital in Kuwait City.

With a lot of cleaning up to do in the aftermath of the attacks and the ever-changing timeline to cross the border into Iraq, we were not able to visit the CSH in Kuwait. Instead, we were forced to get the medical updates by phone.

We were already informed that Captain Seifert had died shortly after getting to the hospital. We had been shocked to hear the news.

"Because he responded so clearly when I spoke with him, I didn't dream that he was hurt so bad that he'd be gone so quickly," Hodges said to me in hushed tones.

Even as we mourned the loss of one of our best soldiers, we had to turn our attention to our wounded warriors still being treated.

Captain Wisher was suffering from severe internal injuries, as well as injuries to his leg. Not knowing the gravity of his own injuries while in the field, Wisher had worked on his friend Stone's more serious wounds, ignoring his own for as long as he could stand it.

Once he and Stone were taken to the aid station—even before being medevac'd to the CSH in Kuwait—Wisher was told his lung had collapsed. He received a shot of Novocain just as a two-inch cut was made so they could insert a tube into his chest.

Now that he was in Kuwait, he seemed to be recouping as well as could be expected.

Armosolo would be transferred to Germany and then on to Walter Reed Medical Center in Washington, DC. He would return to Fort Campbell, KY, and eventually be sent to the San Diego Medical Center in Southern California to recover closer to his family. He would, however, never return to deployable status on active duty.

Next we checked on Major Romaine. His surgery was now complete.

They cleaned everything out but didn't really close anything up. He had been shot through the left hand; it was just kind of hanging on by the skin. The bullet went through the bone of the hand and then through his leg. Luckily the bullet just went straight through his leg and didn't hit any bones or arteries.

As our injured were recovering, the rumor that a U.S. Soldier had committed the attack was winding its way through the hospital. Romaine assumed that it was an attack by Iraqi forces, but he learned the truth just as he was emerging from the anesthesia.

"I can't believe what happened to you guys," a nurse said to Romaine.

"What are you talking about?" he said. "We're at war. Why can't you believe that someone would get shot?"

The nurse realized she should not have said anything, and began to walk away.

"What do you mean by that?" Romaine demanded.

"Well, because of who was responsible and how it happened," the nurse said.

"I don't know what you're talking about," Romaine replied.

Another staffer jumped in and said, "We heard that it was a U.S. soldier who did it."

Romaine had to lay there in recovery far away from the unit, with none of his comrades around, pondering rumors of what happened. Not knowing who it was, he felt alone and very confused.

* * *

Holden and Stone were among those in Camp Udari who would need to be in stable condition before they could make the bumpy helicopter flight that would transport them to the CSH in Kuwait City. There they would join Wisher, Romaine, and Armosolo for further treatment.

The Kuwait City field hospital would be a turning point for our wounded. Those who could be treated here and deemed "combat ready" would return to the front lines with the rest of us in the Bastogne Brigade. The others would board a medical airplane to be evacuated to Landstuhl Regional Medical Center in Rhineland, Germany, which was equipped to handle more severe injuries. Landstuhl was the largest U.S. military hospital outside of the continental United States, and the nearest treatment center for wounded soldiers to come out of Iraq.

After several cancellations, the plane to Germany finally arrived to take back the first round of the wounded. Romaine was aboard the first flight back.

Holden would miss that first flight out of Kuwait. He ultimately had two more surgeries in the field before he caught a later flight to Germany.

On the first medevac plane to Germany, a public affairs person onboard informed everyone of the commotion they would face upon landing.

"You guys are the first service members injured returning back from OIF (Operation Iraqi Freedom) 1," he told them. "The media will be there in a crazy frenzy. It's going to be a big deal. So talk about your experience."

The media were particularly interested in Romaine's story. He was asked if he wanted his family flown in for a big interview. In a word, he told them, "No." A Marine ultimately took Romaine's place in the news.

After spending about three days in Germany, Romaine left on the first plane back to the United States. He was among the first to arrive at Andrews Air Force Base. Once again he was greeted with an onslaught of news media as he boarded the bus for Walter Reed Medical Center.

It seemed as though every doctor in the hospital was on duty for the arrival of the wounded that night—about one doctor and two nurses for every one patient. Romaine joked at the excessive staffing, saying to one of the doctors, "I hope we get some assistance tomorrow because it looks like everyone is here tonight."

In the days to follow, a parade of VIPs from Capitol Hill and the Pentagon visited the wounded at Walter Reed Medical Center. Senators and Congressmen visited the injured service members and presented them with coins of appreciation for their sacrifice and their service. The civilian leadership at the Pentagon also breezed through, giving the standard, "Thank you," to each wounded soldier.

In contrast, Army Chief of Staff General Eric Shinseki spent a little more time with each wounded warrior. He spent a long time with Romaine and his family as a special favor to Lieutenant General Richard A. Cody, who had known Romaine from his time as Commander of the 101st Airborne Division.

Romaine's mother was so excited to see the General that she asked for a photo with him. She would hang the picture of her with her arms wrapped around both her son and the General for years to come.

Shinseki, also a wounded vet, told Romaine about his personal struggles with his wounds. He went on to say that this low point did not hinder his career. He was now the highest-ranking military officer in the U.S. Army. Romaine said this personal visit and talk meant a lot to him.

Just as Romaine went through his last surgery at Walter Reed, he was told that his buddy, Captain Chris Seifert, would be buried in Easton, PA.

Hodges, still on the front lines in Iraq, asked a good friend to see if Romaine was willing to attend despite his wounds. Romaine was touched by the gesture.

"I'm honored to do it," Romaine said.

His doctor approved, the staff loaded him up with painkillers, and his wife helped them stuff Romaine in the back seat of their car for the drive to Pennsylvania.

Romaine took a Purple Heart award in its case with him. He presented the case and the ribbon to Terri Seifert, the Captain's bride, and buried the medal with him to honor his sacrifice.

Unfortunately, the Army never officially awarded the Purple Heart to Captain Seifert or any of the servicemen and women who were killed or injured that day in the desert. The award is presented for, "Being wounded or killed in any action against an enemy of the United States or as a result of an act of any such enemy or opposing armed forces." The Army stands firm that an Embedded Enemy does not fall into the exact wording of the definition.

I strongly disagree. The admittance to responsibility, and the self declaration as an opposing force, clearly names Akbar as the antagonistic enemy described in the definition. By that very definition, that same enemy killed and wounded our service members, and therefore, the award of the Purple Heart for their sacrifice is warranted, in my opinion.

* * *

Holden arrived at Walter Reed Medical Center on April 1, 2003. He would not have the same reception as Romaine and the others did who were on that first flight to Germany and then onto Washington, DC.

It was at Walter Reed that Holden first heard two disturbing truths—first, he had been shot and hit by shrapnel from grenades, and second, an American Soldier was the suspected shooter.

In the first 17 days, including the very first day at Camp Udari in Kuwait, Holden would have a total of 11 surgeries. His body fought hard to keep its limbs despite the doctor's claim in Landstuhl that with 100 percent certainty Holden's leg would be amputated.

Romaine would work equally hard to be reinstated, only to have his body betray him.

He convinced the hospital Commander at Fort Campbell to clear him for duty just in time to return to Iraq following the July Fourth weekend. It was great to see him again at Division Headquarters in Iraq. Unfortunately, by September his hand muscles began to atrophy and he had to be put on a plane back to the States. By October, he was set up for surgery at Vanderbilt Hospital in Nashville, TN.

They took a nerve out of his arm and put it in his hand, in hopes that it would regenerate and connect with the other nerve and then grow to innervate the muscle so that he could regain strength. However, his hands never fully recovered. He eventually was assigned to work in the redeployment cell at the Division Headquarters–Rear. He was responsible for the redeployment schedules and the welcome home ceremonies of the returning units.

* * *

We headed back to Camp Pennsylvania with our combat-ready soldiers piled into three Hummers as our more severely wounded were being tended at the field hospitals.

The ride back was full of the chatter we lacked on the way over. As we arrived, the guards lifted the cross gate and we rolled back through the Figure S, back to work.

Just as we dropped everyone off at the Command Center, the CID agent to whom I had told my story before I left for the field hospital approached me. He said that they had since discovered that two grenades had been tossed into my tent, not just one. I had seen the smoking incendiary grenade but in the confusion had not realized a second fragmentary grenade had also been tossed into the tent.

He wanted to take me back to the tent and show me what happened.

As we slowly walked back, I had to get emotionally ready to re-enter my tent and view the destruction for the first time since it had happened.

We proceeded to the step of the wooden plank that was the vestibule. The splatter of Romaine's blood from the gunshot immediately caught my attention. I followed the droplets to a bigger puddle of blood. I carefully stepped over and around it all so as not to disturb it.

The CID agent flung open the flap and the bright, sunny outside light filled the front portion of the tent. Everything began to happen in slow motion. Every single detail seemed to stop in time for me to absorb it all.

I looked to the place where the incendiary grenade exploded. The television where I watched Tiger play was full of ash dust from the smoke. My 9mm ammunition that I inadvertently left behind had not exploded as I feared. It lay there, covered in the black powder.

That first, smoking grenade had burned a gaping hole, about two to three feet wide and just above chest high, on my side of the tent. All of the items along that side were burned to a crisp.

"This is what saved you from injury coming down the aisle," the agent said, pointing to the packed cases of supplies that we had readied for our deployment into Iraq.

The cases of water had exploded or melted with the plastic bottles all over the place, and the wooden pallets were still wet. An MRE box was shredded with the goods emptied onto the floor.

The two duffle bags that I had packed with my own gear had moved a bit from their original space and had little rips in them from the shrapnel. I could not even remember what the contents were. It seemed to have little significance at that point. I rubbed my hand gingerly across one of them and small pieces of shrapnel fell to the floor.

"Here you go, Sergeant Major," the Agent said, directing my attention to where the fragmentary grenade had exploded.

My eyes must have been the size of one of Tiger's golf balls. I stared at a depression about the size of a cantaloupe in the tent's floor. Three feet to the left, the tent's wall and roof had about 100 small holes that let the sunlight through.

A field table that was in my bunk area had been thrown against the wall. It too was splintered with about 50 shrapnel holes. The plastic partition that separated the two areas had been blown apart and was long gone. The locker that Burns had confiscated for me was in three pieces, one of which came to rest on top of my sleeping mat where my head would have been had I not been up watching golf.

My bivy sack, an outer liner to the sleeping bag, was full of holes at the top where your head fits perfectly when sleeping. I always slept with my head snuggly at the top. Shrapnel also ripped the air out of the thin mattress where my body would have laid.

I moved to the middle of what used to be the tent's center aisle and looked into Romaine's area. It seemed oddly undisturbed from the explosion or the fire.

Hodge's chair was full of blood. It had dried a bit, but a puddle still remained in the center of the chair. The floor immediately underneath his chair and near his sleeping mat also contained blood spatters. About seven small pieces of shrapnel in a tight circle had penetrated the partition between my sleeping area and his. Two of those pieces had just been removed from his arm.

Now looking left near the table, I noticed that our unit colors had been burned. The colors are carried into battle to identify us as a unit and to show the unit heritage and history. They had caught fire and now they were destroyed. I just stared at them before bending over to pick them up and dust off what was left.

"Where's Akbar?" I asked the agent.

"We moved him from everyone's sight," the Agent replied.

"Don't tell me where he is," I replied as I felt my anger rise.

As we walked out of what remained of my tent, the sunlight and fresh air hit my face. It was good to be out of the violent crime chamber.

I exited the vestibule and walked straight to Staff Sergeant Gray who was still guarding Akbar's weapon and the empty brass rifle casings. I was still trying to put the pieces together for myself and wanted to see the exit holes of the shrapnel on that side of the tent.

My eyes were focused on the ground just past where the expended brass lay on the ground. It was then that I first noticed a speed loader. Akbar must have loaded the rounds into the magazine on that side of the tent right before shooting Romaine.

That explained why I was able to exit the tent without being shot by Akbar. I had fled a split second before he was ready to shoot.

I continued to follow the shrapnel holes along the side of the tent and saw a small bit of blood there.

Apparently, Akbar threw the second grenade into the tent from the vestibule instead of rolling it under the flap as he did the first grenade. In an attempt to get out of the way of the blast, Akbar must have run to the side of the tent to avoid facing it. However, he chose the wrong side and injured his leg when the shrapnel cut through the tent wall.

I walked to the other side of the tent—the burned side—to see what it looked like from the outside. The first thing I saw was the satellite dish that brought me Tiger Woods and the Bay Hill Invitational golf tournament. Right beside the dish was an empty bandoleer. Akbar discarded it there after removing all of the ammunition from it.

The CID agents were in for a gold mine of evidence. The agent took the necessary steps to release Staff Sergeant Gray from the guarding of Akbar's weapon and expended brass as he began his collection.

It had only been 10 hours, just a mere half a day's work for a deployed soldier.

* * *

General Petraeus arrived at the camp to take a look at the crime scene and assess the situation.

"No one should have to go through anything like this," he said to Hodges.

During this visit, the General was likely evaluating us to ensure that we were still mentally ready to go into combat.

Hodges felt very confident that we were ready to go. As the Commander, he thought his focus now should be on the continued preparation of his soldiers for combat.

By the time the General arrived, Hodges had changed clothes and gotten rid of the bloody boots, pants, and T-shirt and destroyed them. He didn't think that it would be helpful for soldiers to see him walking around covered in blood. He was pleased to see soldiers doing the right thing, continuing to pack up their gear and get their vehicles ready for the invasion into Iraq.

Hodges and I began to discuss Alpha Company 326 Engineers, Akbar's Company. They were obviously unhappy, upset, and ashamed that the perpetrator of this violence was from their company.

"This was an isolated incident by one rogue man," Hodges told them. "There were no signs and no way that you could have known."

As we left, you could see the relief on their faces knowing that they were still very key and essential, a part of the team.

As Hodges and I toured the camp after General Petraeus left, the CID agents were wrapping up a part of the investigation.

They informed me that they soon would be finished taking photographs and marking things inside the tents. Once they were done, they wanted the occupants of the three tents to remove all of their belongings.

I took care of my whole tent, organizing the items into three separate areas. The Colonel had better things to do than clear his tent and Major Romaine was recuperating in a hospital.

I felt like throwing most of my gear away even though I knew I would need it later. Shrapnel permeated my clothes, and that which did not was full of soot and ash from the fire. Everything smelled like a chimney.

Shrapnel was the least of my worries as I packed up the Colonel's area. I had to dance around the blood in his area, trying to salvage as much as possible.

Until then, I had not looked into the Majors' or the Captains' tents to see the impact there. So I decided to go check them out before most of the items were removed. I couldn't believe my eyes. Both of them wore the scars of the violence from just 12 hours prior, and the damage was ten times the amount sustained in my tent.

As I emerged from the tent cleanup, a few reporters sidled up to me to ask a few more questions. After giving them a brief update and some names of people they could interview, I felt like it would be a good time for a nap. Unfortunately, I was wide awake.

My mind was racing. It was just hitting me how really lucky I was to be alive, how Tiger Woods and golf had saved my life. Just a week or so prior, I had an opportunity to watch golf in our tent but passed on it because Tiger wasn't playing. I marvel to this day at how big of an impact such little decisions can make.

As I thought about what needed to be done before we crossed the Iraqi border, I decided now would be a good time to call my mother to assure her that I was okay. She was an avid Dan Rather fan and had no doubt seen the news. I was able to quickly get a call out from Command Center. The phone rang only twice before she picked up.

Even though my mom was aging, she was still quick, gifted, and hip. She was so glad to hear that I was doing well, and let me know that I had called just in time.

"WBNS (the local CBS affiliate in Columbus, OH) is coming to the house to interview me," she said with a cheery voice. "They called me earlier and they'll be here this afternoon, and then it will be on the evening news at six o'clock. Ha, how do you like them apples?"

"You did hear me say that we were attacked, right?" I asked, feeling the need to reiterate that we were attacked and that I was okay.

"Yeah, I heard you boy," she said.

I was not sure that I liked them apples, but I wished her well in her television debut.

* * *

We soon received word that the timeline for our participation in the war had been moved up to Tuesday, which was less than 48 hours away. The confirmation that we were combat ready and that the date had been set was the best news of the day. It was exactly what we needed as a unit.

The TOC was buzzing with the latest news and the sense of urgency to update everything. Some soldiers still needed to write their statements. The agents were tracking them down.

Multitasking was at its highest level. Between current operations, the intensified future operations, preparation of statements, and the post attack clean up and restoration, there was much to accomplish in a short time.

We were left with only one day to execute a memorial service for Seifert. It was much too late to do it that day, which meant it had to be first thing the next day, Monday. I approached the Colonel and we briefly discussed what we wanted to do.

"I want it like The Old Guard," Hodges said, which meant the highest ceremonial standard.

That was all I needed to hear.

Before the sun went down, it was decided that the occupants of the attacked tents would move all of their belongings into the supply tent.

Now that it was clear one of our own had attacked us, I no longer trusted a person just because they wore the same uniform as I did. Those days were now gone.

Therefore, I asked something from our soldiers that I had never asked before; I asked that a platoon of our own Infantrymen guard the supply tent and the Headquarters area.

The television in my old tent had been moved into the one of the adjoining tents of the TOC. The final round of the Bay Hill Invitational golf tournament was on. I felt it only fitting that I pay homage to Tiger by watching him play. After all, he merely saved my life.

I found a chair and placed it right in front of the TV—the best seat in the house. Tiger had a seven-stroke lead and no one was going to catch him!

Others gathered around and a few pulled up a chair to cheer for the leader. If only for a few hours, golf had given us a welcome distraction. The tournament concluded and Tiger won by a swopping 11 strokes for his fourth consecutive Bay Hill victory. I felt lucky to have witnessed it.

It was now 0430 hours. I closed my eyes and reviewed the sequence of Seifert's memorial service so that it would be fresh in my mind the next day . . . or rather in a few hours; then I dozed right off.

* * *

In no time, I heard alarms going off and people moving around. I was scared to look at my watch for fear it was way too early to get up and that I had only gotten one hour of sleep. I continued to lay there until someone said, "Sergeant Major, it's zero six thirty. We have the Memorial Service at zero eight hundred."

I did sleep more than an hour, two to be exact. I had at least gotten some rest and still had enough time to check on the progress of the memorial service preparation and gobble down a quick breakfast. Working off of fumes, from the events and pace of the past two days, I still felt sharp and energized to supervise the best send off for Captain Christopher Seifert.

The goal of such a memorial service is to replicate and render honor to the fallen as close to that of a traditional funeral in Arlington National Cemetery as possible.

A mock cenotaph-like structure was erected, composed of Seifert's boots and placed in front of sandbags that were used instead of a stand to mount his weapon. The weapon was turned upside down with the bayonet fixed, stuck into the sandbags for support. His helmet, adorned with the coveted club on each side, was positioned on top of the butt stock of the weapon, and his dog tags, hanging by its chain, were draped across the length of the rifle. The toes of the boots and the front of the helmet both faced the audience, or in this case, where the troops would be standing for the ceremony. This mock cenotaph-like structure was on display as remains in a casket would be for viewing.

There is never a good time for an emotional event like this, but it is critically important to pause and pay respect for the soldier's ultimate sacrifice to their service, honor, and country. We were thankful that we did not have more pairs of boots on display.

Hedrick narrated the ceremony. The Chaplain led the much-needed prayer. And Warren shared personal remarks about an extraordinary and promising life cut far too short. I was the Commander of Troops, a task that Romaine would have normally done.

The rest of the Headquarters Company gathered in the open gravel area near the TOC. Surrounded by the Texas barriers, configured in a 10-by-10 meter square perimeter, it was the perfect location for the memorial service. It was the same area that many of us had fled to just two nights before, including Akbar, to defend ourselves and our comrades from the invasion of the enemy.

Unit by unit, 50 members of each Battalion positioned themselves in a horseshoe surrounding the mock cenotaph.

General Petraeus arrived with Command Sergeant Major Hill and a few others from the Division staff to pay their respects.

"The best thing we can do to respect Chris as a father, a soldier, and a comrade is to get on our horses and get ready to go into this fight and to win," Warren said, referring to the fight in Iraq. He felt that this was a critical point to make as we were just hours from loading our trucks and helicopters to head toward the border.

"Bastogne, Attention. Present Arms," I commanded. The units were called to the position of attention, to present arms and to render honors of the 21-gun salute. Seven soldiers with M4 rifles and the NCO in Charge stood just on the outside of the Texas barriers near the perimeter wall to fire the rounds over the mock cenotaph.

Even among the most brave and stoic soldiers in attendance, you would have been hard pressed to find one dry eye as the ceremony ended with the playing of Taps.

Petraeus, the Commanding General, led the paying of respects to Captain Seifert. He stepped up to the mock cenotaph. Colonel Hodges followed with Hill, Warren, the Brigade Staff, Battalion Commanders, and eventually most in attendance.

As a gesture of final respect, some saluted, Commanders placed their coveted challenge coins on the sandbags, some gingerly touched the helmet as if it were Captain Seifert's casket, some got down on one knee and crossed their heart, and some just walked by slowing looking at the helmet and weapon.

A few groups of two or three stood at the cenotaph in tears, while others stood off to the side doing the same. Most telling was the group of three Captains—Williams, Sabatini, and Place,

Akbar's Company Commander. The three had their arms around each other's shoulders consoling one another. All a part of the grieving process.

It was a sad and somber moment. Yet in a couple of hours we would be back to the task at hand, prepping for our journey into war.

CHAPTER 10
Wounded Invasion

Less than 60 hours after the attack began and 24 hours after Captain Seifert's memorial service, the Bastogne Brigade had its long-awaited orders to join the fight in Iraq. With heavy hearts, a strong resolve, and eight fewer warfighters, we limped into Iraq.

We drove all day and all night in what is known as a Ground Assault Convoy. Soldiers were on the backs of trucks doing their best to remain in a protective postured position by facing outward with their weapons pointed away from the vehicle. The terrain was rough, not the smooth ride we expected in the desert. Not even the padded seats could soften the sharp, repetitive jolts to the spine.

Ahead of us lay Highway One that ran from Kuwait to points north to Baghdad and beyond. Our intelligence suggested that it would be lined with Iraqi armor. All I could hear in my head was Hodges saying, "If you look like a duck, they'll treat you like a duck." And we would have been sitting ducks had we taken that road.

Focused on relieving the Battalion from 3rd Brigade that was already positioned out in the middle of the desert, Hodges was determined to make good time. They were securing the Forward Area Refueling Point for the Blackhawk and Apache helicopters.

He remembered from his time in 3rd Battalion, 187th Infantry, how a bunch of the Vietnam veterans from that unit still badmouthed some of the 506th Infantry Curahees. The 187th veterans felt strongly that it had taken the Curahees far too long to reach them and help them fight off the enemy on Hamburger Hill. The 187th still blamed the excessive loss of life at that battle on the Curahees.

It struck a chord with Hodges that more than 30 years later the vets were still angry. So in his mind there was no way that he was going to allow this group of 3rd Brigade soldiers to sit out there and talk trash about us 30 years later.

The coalition force, though equipped with Unmanned Aerial Vehicles (also known as UAVs or drones) was not a priority to our convoy route. Therefore, we were not certain of the location of any threat from Iraqi forces.

Worst-case scenario would be that an Iraqi armored force rolled up on the Battalion of 3rd Brigade, leaving ground soldiers to fight tanks. We could not let that happen.

* * *

A Brigade Combat Team without the Executive Officer is the equivalent of the New England Patriots without Tom Brady. Iraq was our Super Bowl, and here we were without Major Romaine.

In addition to no Romaine, we had no interpreters. After having been suspected of terrorism, they had politely declined our offer to join us in battle.

Nevertheless, we were determined to win no matter how many people had to play offense, defense, and special teams. Hodges felt confident that our second- and third-level teammates could accomplish the mission without the starters.

Captain Roman Rubalcaba moved to the position of the Headquarters Company Commander. The young officer who was just a year removed from being a Platoon leader prepared to do his best filling in for Holden who—without question—was irreplaceable.

I was asked to be the new Executive Officer. Even with all of my experience, I was no match for Romaine's skills as a combat operations tactician.

At precisely 0800 hours with our new leadership in place, the front of the long line of vehicles began to roll, taking the First Brigade Combat Team toward the border and into combat.

I wanted to look back at my tent one last time but thought it best that it be in the rearview mirror. I had to leave the attack behind so I could focus on our new journey and our new enemy.

Our brethren in the 2nd and 3rd Brigades were not going to be let down. The Bastogne Brigade would be there next to them to write history.

Although proud that we were able to move out on time, Hodges soon realized how much we were struggling without Romaine and Holden. They would have been the two main people responsible for moving this convoy.

The combination of the losses of these two integral players, the arduous road conditions, and a sleep-deprived combat team quickly led to frustration.

The Battalion's Commanders kept urging Hodges to slow down the front vehicles because their speed was causing dangerous breaks in contact. The big gaps between vehicles happened all night.

"Keep up, we're not stopping," Hodges said. "Keep moving!"

We had just been issued the BLUFOR Tracker, a state-of-the-art GPS device with a 19-inch screen affixed to the Hummers. We had been trained on the technology in simulation, but this was our first time putting it to use in this environment. To add to the challenge, the entire Combat Team had only three devices issued for use with well over 200 vehicles.

The convoy adventure continued well into the morning with only a few rest breaks, none of which were enough to fully recuperate. All of the qualified drivers went through the gambit of constantly switching out to stay as fresh as possible.

We finally halted for a much-needed sleep break around 0300, about 21 hours after we started out. Security was put in place with a rotation plan to protect us from an Iraqi onslaught while we slept.

Three short hours later, calls on our vehicle's radio set woke everyone. We started moving again.

We stayed on the road taking short 20-minute breaks until 1600 hours when we halted to rest for the night. We unloaded the trucks and got settled into our resting place for the next 12 hours.

Hodges had no idea that the ride was going to be as hard as it had been. We were relieved to be able to sit on the ground and eat an MRE without bobbling all around in the confines of a truck.

I had barely opened my MRE when I was summoned to meet Colonel Hodges by his truck for what appeared to be some sort of meeting of the senior leadership. Hodges informed us that although Major Stone had fought one tough battle for his life, he didn't make it.

Our inner circle of leaders moved closer to pause for a moment of silence and prayer.

Just fresh into enemy territory, the short reflection and remembrance was the best memorial service tribute that we could provide.

* * *

We were up bright and early and on the road again for our second full day of driving. Late in the evening we arrived just short of our final location to bed down.

At first light on day three of our treacherous drive, a recon party was sent to find the exact location of our new temporary home.

Our friends from the 3rd Infantry Division had been in the area for a few days and assisted in scouting a suitable area. Within a few hours we descended upon a small schoolhouse complex that had an adjoining residential house.

The area, several kilometers from any other dwelling, was large enough for the Brigade Headquarters and all of its vehicles.

The Headquarters Company spread out throughout the school and the house. The school had eight classrooms, some with chairs and chalkboards. The floors were made of crumbling concrete. It was hard to fathom how a child could learn in an environment like that.

A few days passed and we quickly became accustomed to our new surroundings. It was hot by day and less hot by night here in the outskirts of Najef, Iraq.

I was failing as the Brigade's Executive Officer. It was becoming painfully clear how much Romaine was needed. I was not used to focusing on every aspect of the command center. My concern had always been on soldiers and not on operations.

When Lieutenant Colonel Jon Lehr showed up in our new space in the Iraqi desert, I was greatly relieved. Just eight short months ago, Lehr had Commanded the 3-327 Infantry Battalion. He was very familiar with the Brigade and how it operated.

I knew him well, and it was good to see him again and work with him as our new Brigade Executive Officer. Smiles from Hodges and the staff could not have been larger as he emerged into the new Command Center near the school.

Shortly thereafter, we received two more critical replacements—a JAG Officer, Major Roger Nell, and an Intelligence Officer, Captain Brian Hayes. Both were quickly integrated into the Bastogne Brigade Headquarters.

* * *

We began to gain a foothold in the City of Najef after fighting off the attacks of a few insurgents hostile to the Coalition. We crept forward, securing different parts of the city from all directions.

Once we had control of the town, the Headquarters was moved forward into an abandoned condo complex. We had no electricity and slow running water on the days that we had any at all.

It was clear that families had only recently fled, upon news of a war. Clothes, furniture, and other household items were left behind. They must have stuffed as many bags as possible before hitting the road.

We told our soldiers to be respectful of their property and belongings. We knew the families would move back in as soon as peace resumed.

The condo that the Commander, the Executive Officer, and I shared with the drivers had a living room, a small dining room, two bedrooms, a kitchen, and a bathroom. A small foyer greeted visitors, and stairs from the inside lead to an open-air rooftop that had a balcony.

Hodges and I slept on the balcony despite it being a bit dangerous and unprotected. It was nice and cool and provided somewhat fresher air than inside the condo, especially given the only occasional opportunity to take a shower. I had already been caught several times in the shower when the water stopped flowing, and I had to use bottled water to finish the job.

We were as "settled in" as anyone can be in enemy territory. You have to be hyper-vigilant to stay alive there.

As I left the condo on my way to dinner one night, a soldier I did not recognize entered.

"Who lives here?" he asked.

Until that moment, I had all but forgotten the theory that

Akbar had an accomplice. This odd exchange made that story come flooding back to me.

"What are you doing here," I demanded.

"I was just looking around," he explained.

"Get the hell out of here, and don't you ever come back looking around," I said with a low, angry voice. "Do you understand?"

"Roger, Sergeant Major," he replied as he backed out of our space.

I later discovered that he was assigned to our Field Artillery unit. While that meant he was from a different unit than Akbar, they still could have been buddies while off duty.

A few nights had passed when again I heard someone creeping into the condo foyer. It was almost the exact same time of day as the earlier incident.

I stood in a dark spot, then slowly drew my 9mm out of its holster and cocked it. Once the person got close enough, I stuck the barrel of my weapon into his chest.

"Freeze," I yelled.

Just then, I saw the white envelope of mail. It was a Staff Sergeant delivering the mail.

"Damn, Sergeant Major," the Staff Sergeant said in frightened disbelief.

I apologized and tried to quickly explain the earlier prowler and how Burns thought that Akbar had an accomplice.

Even though the Staff Sergeant knew the story, he still was not pleased to have a loaded and cocked 9mm aimed at his chest, even if he did have his armored vest on.

Concerns about PTSD started to haunt me. I found it hard to tell anyone about that night. I was unsure how to tell everyone to stay away from me, especially in the dark, because I no longer trusted my fellow soldiers.

* * *

Almost three weeks after we arrived in Najef, our Battalion units left the Headquarters and were spread out across Iraq. Soon our media crew left, transported to Baghdad, and then headed back to the States.

Having shrunk dramatically, our Headquarters relocated to a secluded, beautiful little oasis surrounded with tall palm trees and calf-high, soft grass. You could hear the animals from the neighboring farms, but that was as close as we got to civilization.

As we settled into our new quarters, we began to take stock of what we had. The Executive Officer of the Aviation Brigade asked Warren how he was doing. Warren said he was a little tired and that he planned to inform the Commander that he needed to get a couple hours of rest. The XO said, "Well you look like you need it."

"What I really need is some is some underwear and T-shirts," Warren said. "All I've had with me the last few weeks were the pair I have on and one extra that was in my assault pack."

Since Warren's sleep area had taken a direct hit in the grenade attack, he had no sleeping bag, few uniforms, no underwear, and only limited gear. We had not even had time to notice that every few days Warren was washing his clothes in a bucket.

The Executive Officer had just gotten a package from home that had brand new packs of underwear and T-shirts.

"I just got these in the mail, you can have them," he said.

Warren was happy to get some fresh, clean underclothes. He took a shower and couldn't wait to put them on. He did not even care that he had shrunk to a 28-inch waist, and the underwear was a size 42.

* * *

With the Battalions spread out, Hodges and I would visit two Battalions a day, logging many miles in dangerous territory.

One night, when we were still in the cozy oasis, Hodges walked alone, deep into the palm trees. He found a safe place and bawled his eyes out. It was the first time that he had a chance to grieve over the loss of his men, Captain Chris Seifert and Major Greg Stone. He was despondent over the whole attack.

It was then that I realized that we had been inseparable since we left Camp Pennsylvania. Cramped quarters and Hummers do not allow for much privacy. We had been busy with mission after mission with no personal time at all.

We had not talked about that night. No one talked about it. It was not the type of story where people sat around saying, "Remember that time." Everyone continued to deal with it in their own way, mostly by carrying on with the business of combating the enemy.

* * *

We left the tranquil setting of the oasis and headed to Baghdad and then to locations north of Baghdad.

Travelling on paved road surfaces made the journey a cinch compared to our first convoy. After two days, we arrived at our destination, an old Iraqi Air Base just west of the town of

Qayyarah. We named the Forward Operating Base—what would be our new home for the remainder of our yearlong tour in Iraq—Q-West.

On the first day, Hodges and I flew over the area that was to be our responsibility. It was gigantic. We lost one Infantry Battalion when it was detached from us and moved over to 2nd Brigade, so we were down quite a few warfighters. We would have to do more with less.

An ammo supply point at least as large as seven football fields was in our area. As we flew by, rounds and rounds of rockets were visible, along with containers of ammunition for rifles. We knew that if the insurgents ever got their hands on that stuff and knew how to use it correctly, we were in serious trouble.

The next day we flew to a town in western Iraq on the border of Syria. No U.S. forces were up there, and we were tasked to put a company there until the 3rd Brigade could make it up from Baghdad. We were so close that you could walk to Syria. So I did.

The border guard came out of his guard shack, smiling and armed with a stick, to greet the five of us who were all heavily armed with M4 rifles and 9mm pistols. I gestured that I wanted to step across the line. He just smiled. I went to the line, walked across, looked around at the desolate surroundings, and walked back across.

* * *

Within a couple of months of arriving at Q-West in Iraq, we became a part of the surrounding community. We wanted to "win the hearts and minds" of our neighbors so that we could avoid any more bloodshed.

We established police stations and schools, helped re-open a construction plant, and extinguished a massive fire at a major sulfur plant, saving the lives of many local villagers. Our firefighting efforts reached NBC's Tom Brokaw who came to an award ceremony in Iraq that recognized the valiant efforts of the local fire fighters and volunteers for their heroic service.

We also held a huge gathering on the base for the nearby town's influential leaders and their families. We wanted to show them that we were there to help with progress and not to hinder it. We displayed our capabilities and weaponry in a county fair-like atmosphere.

Our night vision devices had drawn a lot of attention before this event. It was rumored they were "magical" and enabled the viewer to look through the clothing of women. As we drove through the streets, the citizens would run to a covered area to avoid being seen.

To set the record straight at our event, we set up a darkened tent and allowed the men to check out the device for themselves. They quickly learned that the devices were not that magical after all, finding the notion as hilarious as we had all along.

* * *

After a long year in Iraq, it was time to redeploy back to Fort Campbell. Despite Akbar's accusations, no women were raped and no children were killed by members of the Bastogne Brigade Combat Team.

CHAPTER 11
Justice

The Bastogne Brigade was nothing if not patient and determined to see justice.

We had waited more than 800 days after the September 11, 2001, attacks on our nation's soil to make it to the border of Iraq to help exact justice on our enemy.

Now, just short of 800 days, we were finally going to see justice for the March 23, 2003, attack on our comrades by a fellow soldier.

It was April 2005 when the court martial of Army Sergeant Hasan Akbar finally began in Fort Bragg, NC.

* * *

A court martial is an odd place for a reunion, but you take what you can get in the Army.

Just over one year after we wrapped up our tour of duty in Iraq, and two years after the grenade attacks in our little spot in the Kuwaiti desert, the soldiers of Bastogne Brigade were brought together again on the eve of the Akbar trial.

The date was finally set for April 11, 2005. Akbar's defense entered an insanity plea almost immediately, therefore drawing things out. Every day we waited was another day that kept our wounds fresh.

It was also hard for those of us with battle scars to swallow that Akbar continued to receive full pay throughout the trial —from American taxpayer dollars—as a Sergeant in the United States Army. This was a man who had killed two and wounded a dozen more of his fellow soldiers whom he had sworn to protect.

The flow of American cash did not even stop after his second attack on an American soldier while awaiting trial.

One day when Akbar was in counsel with his attorney, he snuck a pair of scissors out of the office. As he was being escorted back to his cell by the Military Police, Akbar brutally stabbed one of the guards in the neck.

The guard survived the attack, but the Judge for the case would not allow that attack to be used as evidence in the trial for the grenade attack. That premeditated attack on the Military Police could have thrown a huge curveball at the insanity plea for the grenade attack. It might have helped show a pattern of opportunistically planned and premeditated attacks on U.S. soldiers.

* * *

I was one of the last soldiers still at Fort Campbell when the trial began. Air-Butler had retired and now worked for me at the NCO Academy as a civilian. We each made the 615-mile trek to Fort Bragg, NC, alone.

The Judge Advocate General, or JAG, wanted me to report to their offices on base at Fort Bragg the evening before the trial to set up a time to prepare me for testimony. Everyone had a scheduled time to be prepped. So when I visited their office, I snuck a peek at the list to get an idea of whom I would see at the trial.

After my briefing, I left the Advocate's office and checked into the hotel about 10 miles away from base where the court martial would be held. I was glad to find First Sergeant Stevenson, Sergeant First Class Burns, and Captain Holden already gathered in Burns's room. It was awesome to see them again.

We sat around and caught up on each other's lives. I informed them that I had submitted my paperwork to retire, and it was approved. In less than three months, I would be out the door after 29½ years.

They were surprised I was not staying to serve in positions of greater responsibility. I told them that I was happy with my decision. I had joined on my own terms and was departing on my own terms.

The First Sergeant shared his news to do the same in the next few months. It turned out we would be out around the same time.

Holden's injuries kept him from immediately returning to deployable status after the attack. At the time of the trial, he was still working on getting back on track with his health.

The doctors had to remove a portion of his shattered leg and dozens of pieces of shrapnel embedded in his torso. He did keep the promise he made to himself at the beginning of the ordeal—that he would not look at the back of his injured leg for seven months.

Although I initially experienced unease at discussing the past and our futures, that first mini-reunion really helped relieve some of the stress I was feeling as we headed toward the trial.

* * *

Burns, Holden, and I rode together to the office because our prep times with the lawyers were all within 15 minutes of each other.

The prep seemed easy enough. All I had to talk about was what I knew about that night, including all of the events of the attack that were etched into my brain. I believe the truth always prevails, and I was far from being intimidated by anyone. I had testified in trials before. So far my track record was near perfect—most every defendant I testified against had been found guilty. I was hoping my luck would continue.

We left the Advocates' office and found our way onto a local golf course. I was excited to play another round of golf. I had flown with my clubs and looked forward to the opportunity.

I like to walk and the First Sergeant joined me. Holden definitely needed a cart.

He was struggling with his golf shots, but he was able to make a few nice ones. He finally succumbed to the pain after gutting it out on nine holes.

It was painful to watch Holden continue to struggle with his injuries. He did his best to drive on with life, determined to do the things that he loved to do. But it did not look like a long golf drive was in his near future.

In the end, Holden would have 17 surgeries. The last one was to reconstruct his good leg for overcompensating for the injured one. Later, he would defy all the odds by passing the Army Physical Fitness test—and not just passing, but doing so in the 17-21 age group.

He eventually was medically cleared to remain on active duty and in deployable status. He volunteered and was redeployed to Iraq, serving three more tours.

I, on the other hand, would go on to my planned retirement, and continue playing my beloved golf and watching my idol, Tiger Woods. I am forever reminded that if I had not stayed up to watch him on March 23, 2003, I may not be here to play the game today.

* * *

At 0800 hours that Monday morning, we gathered in the waiting room for the case, *United States vs. Hasan Akbar*, to begin.

More of the soldiers and family members from Bastogne Brigade joined Burns, Holden, and me in the waiting area.

Captain Hedrick was one of the first men I saw. He was now stationed at Fort Bragg as the new head of training and operations for an Infantry Battalion in the 82nd Airborne Division. We embraced, very glad to see each other again.

I shared the same enthusiasm upon seeing Major Warren. Though he had left the Brigade and was still at Fort Campbell with the 160th Special Operations Regiment, I had not seen him since our return. Terri Seifert was there to ensure that justice was served. I could only imagine her eagerness for this process to finally begin.

After a few joyful reunions, the room got quiet as the prosecutor read off our names in order of appearance on the witness stand.

This was the first day of testimony, and it would take as long as necessary. Twelve of us were set to testify. After testifying, we were then given the option to remain in the courtroom to listen to the rest of the trial.

The witnesses seemed to move pretty quickly on and off the stand. It looked like those with the shortest testimony were scheduled first. Those of us with more to say had to wait until the end of the day.

I was never very good at waiting. I kept running to get coffee to stay awake, which led to a lot of bathroom breaks. Longing for the taste of Starbucks, I ended up not being able to stomach one more drop of that cheap, office-brewed coffee.

Hedrick was finally called in around 1100 hours. I was scheduled to follow him.

* * *

Before the trial, Hedrick had been in touch online and on the phone with Captain Seifert's widow, Terri Seifert, and several members of Major Stone's family. However, today at the trial was the first time he had seen Mrs. Seifert, so he spent some time with her before he was called in to testify.

He knew that he would be recounting graphic details of that night and wanted her to be prepared. He also wanted her to know that the Captain was surrounded by his buddies at the end, and that he was not alone.

So, Hedrick replayed the events of that night to her in a nearby sports bar on base. He told of hearing the pain that her husband was in, and hearing the voices of the first responders trying to keep him awake as they medevac'd him to the field hospital.

After talking to Mrs. Seifert, he went to the hotel where Major Stone's family was staying and did the same with Stone's mother. Hedrick told her that he still felt awful remembering that night in the tent having written her son Stone off at first glance as unable to save. He still had not forgiven himself.

* * *

Before they could say, "Command Sergeant Major Womack," I was already standing in the door.

As I entered the courtroom, I tried to orient myself. The room was dark, at least much darker than I expected. En route to the witness stand, I passed behind a row of pew-style seats and then turned left down the center aisle.

As I strode down the aisle, I passed by the defense table where the defendant sat at the end, nearest the aisle. The prosecution table was on my right. The entire courtroom was much smaller than the other courts I had seen before.

I stepped up to the stand and quickly took the oath to tell the truth, administered by the prosecuting attorney. The stand that held the 15-member jury, a mix of Senior Noncommissioned Officers and Officers, was directly to my left. The Judge's bench, occupied by a Colonel and perched two feet above my eye level, was immediately to my right. I now faced the courtroom and the attorneys.

As soon as I was sworn in and instructed to take a seat, I immediately began looking for Akbar.

I wanted to see the face of the man who wanted me dead. When I spotted him, all I could see was the top of his head as he looked down at his lap.

The first question was asked. I cannot say exactly what happened, but I know I felt a sense of relief that the trial was at last taking place. Finally, justice seemed tangible.

My eyes moved back toward the prosecutor, dressed in the Army green Class A uniform, asking the question.

I answered him as best I could and then looked at the jury. I wanted to see if I could tell by their faces whether or not they would convict. I looked at their ranks, their ribbons, and back to their faces.

With the next question, my eyes went back to Akbar. I was yearning to make eye contact with him. I wanted him to look at me, to see me. He had not looked at me the night of the attack. He had just rolled a grenade under my tent flap and run like a coward.

Now that I was at his trial, I was getting pissed off that he would not look at me. I must be good enough to kill but not good enough to look at, I thought to myself.

The next few questions came and went. Finally Akbar looked up, and I caught his eyes. I stared directly into them without blinking.

When I was assigned to guard at the Tomb of the Unknown Soldier, I was taught not to blink. I became very good at it. I just stared at him, as if it were only the two of us in the courtroom.

The next few questions came and I answered them while still staring at Akbar. Finally, he looked back down. I felt as if I had won Round 1.

The defense attorney, dressed in his Class As, stood during his cross-examination. I tried to re-engage Akbar in our staring match, but he would not make eye contact with me again.

When I was released from the stand, I chose to remain in the courtroom to watch and listen to the rest of the trial.

I love true crime novels and courtroom drama on television and in the movies. I was hoping to catch some stunning turnaround or interesting story twists, but none happened. The evidence and the testimony were pretty routine and straightforward.

When the judge called for a recess, I saw for the first time that Akbar was shackled by the ankles with a chain that ran up his leg and connected to his handcuffed hands. He shimmied to his feet with the help of the MPs and shuffled in four-inch steps as he was escorted out of the courtroom.

* * *

After three days of testimony, the defense rested. It was now with the jury. With our testimony over, we were allowed to go.

We had one more meal left on our allotted Army per diem, so we thought it fitting to have one last gathering before we went our separate ways.

We found a nice restaurant in Fayetteville, NC, that served a great steak. It was no celebration, but we wanted to treat ourselves.

Our only real plan was to eat. Our rowdy crowd filled a 12-foot table and took over three waiters and two assistants in this tiny establishment. Most of us ordered the biggest steak they had and everyone, except Burns, had a drink in his hand. So Burns became the designated driver.

Everyone was buying each other drinks until we forgot whose turn it was to buy. With the steak on order, Holden sprung for a couple of bottles of red wine. Before we got too carried away, a toast was made in honor of our fallen comrades from the horrific attack that had brought us back together—Captain Chris Seifert and Major Greg Stone.

Dinner was served and lasted for more than four hours. The bar was open, and we migrated across the room to assemble there, closing the place around 0100 hours. No one in the group had to appear in court so everyone could sleep in a bit before catching flights back to their home station.

The next day, as many of us were preparing to fly out, we knew the jury still had to hear a few more days of testimony before it would deliver a verdict.

After a very short deliberation, the jury determined that Akbar acted with premeditation and found him guilty of first-degree murder.

Akbar was found guilty of the murders of Army Captain Christopher Seifert and of Air Force Major Gregory Stone. The first he killed by shooting him in the back and the second died of complications from 83 shrapnel wounds. He was also found guilty of attempted murder for trying to kill as many of us as he could and wounding 12 of us in the process.

* * *

In less than two weeks, most of us were summoned back to Fort Bragg for the death penalty hearing. A new face there that hadn't been at the trial was Colonel Hodges. Although stationed at Fort Bragg, he was in Iraq during the initial trial and had not been called to appear.

It was great to see him again. Besides communicating through a few emails, this was the first time that we had seen each other since his Change of Command almost a year before.

He wanted to see everyone and invited us to gather at his Fort Bragg quarters for dinner. It was a festive time sitting around talking about the good ole days. As was Hodges' custom, he broke out the cigars and the smokers assembled in the backyard. I puffed on them only occasionally, as I don't care for the smoky taste that lingers in my mouth for days.

The sentencing phase was much the same as the trial. The most graphic details of the injuries and the methodical preciseness of the attack were repeated. In addition to the graphic testimony of the events, we were able also to testify about the impact of the deaths of our comrades.

Both men were fathers. Seifert's son was just moving from infancy to toddlerhood. Stone's two sons were just at the age of being able to have fun and learn a bit about life.

Your father is supposed to be your teacher, your mentor, your guide, and your protector. The sons of these men would never be able to say, "My dad taught me. My dad showed me. My dad made me this."

This loss really hit home for me. I had two sons of my own who were close to the same ages as Major Stone's sons. In addition, I was about the age of Captain Seifert's son when my own father died. I knew exactly what they would be missing.

The jury made quick business of their decision. Akbar was sentenced to death by a unanimous vote of the military panel. Those of us left behind were relieved that justice was served.

* * *

In November 2006—more than 18 months after the conviction on charges of premeditated murder and attempted murder—the incumbent Commander of the XVIII Airborne Corps and court martial convening authority in the case, signed the order to execute punishment of the death penalty to Sergeant Hasan Akbar.

The death penalty case automatically goes to appeal and will be reviewed by the U.S. Army Court of Criminal Appeals, the U.S. Court of Appeals for the Armed Forces, and ultimately could end up at the U.S. Supreme Court. Akbar cannot be executed until the President of the United States gives the approval.

To date, 160 members of the Armed Forces have been executed since the death penalty was instituted in 1942. The last execution was on 13 April 1961. Of those, 157 were members of the United States Army.

On July 28, 2008, President George W. Bush approved the first execution since 1961 of United States Army Private Ronald A. Gray. A jury of his peers convicted him in April 1988 for multiple murders and rapes. A month later, the Secretary of the Army Pete Geren set an execution date of December 10, 2008, and ordered that Gray be put to death by lethal injection.

An Army spokesperson announced Gray's execution date on November 20, 2008. However, six days later, on November 26,

Gray was granted a stay of execution by a federal judge to give him time for further appeals. He has not yet been executed as of 2013.

Akbar is next in line, but if history is any indication, it will be a long wait for justice.

EPILOGUE
The Insider Threat - It's closer than you think

E ven as our troops were gearing up to cross the border into
Iraq, Americans were beginning to return to their normal,
daily lives following the September 11, 2001, terrorist attacks.
We were behaving as if we believed those attacks were a fluke and
that it would not—indeed could not—happen again.

Though we acted as though something so horrific could not
happen again, deep inside our innocence was gone, and we knew
that we had to become vigilant. Vigilant, yes, but we would not
let the terrorists win. We would shop. We would go to school.

We would go to the movies, hang out with our friends, and bring donuts into the office on Monday mornings.

We sent our well-trained military over to the Middle East to stop the terrorists before they crossed our borders again.

Ironically, as you just read, even those of us with the best training in the world, those of us laser focused on our target— the terrorists—did not see our own Insider Threat. How could we? After all, Sergeant Akbar's actions constituted the first attack of its kind in American military history. Unfortunately, now we know better, and that is why I shared this story. I will always feel a responsibility to protect my country, but the kind of protection we will need going forward requires each of us to play an active role.

A decade later as I look back on my experience with the benefit of hindsight, in addition to a lengthy trial and hundreds of pages of testimony and interviews, I see patterns emerge and lessons take shape. I feel, therefore, compelled to share what I learned and to provide a wake-up call, because the Insider Threat is closer than you think.

First, let me define "Insider Threat" so we are all talking about the same thing. I see the Insider Threat as a person who is embedded in your life, integrated into the American dream. They are not strangers. They fit in and succeed at looking the same as everyone else. They attend private and public schools at every level, are born and give birth in our hospitals, play sports, go to parties, are technically savvy, and even polite. They'll do whatever it takes in society to be accepted as "just another American." With success, no one can differentiate them, and therefore our guard is let down and the once heightened instincts are lowered—or possibly even turned off.

Often the media, elected officials, and other opinion leaders differentiate between domestic mass murders and terrorists. However, the only real difference is their declaration of allegiance to a known terrorist organization. In reality, they are the same threat to our American way of life, one of freedom and a host of cultures. One thing I have learned from my experience and the time since March 23, 2003, is that these threats are one and the same—they are the Insider Threat.

If you are maimed, or a loved one is killed, you likely do not care if the killer was a disgruntled employee or a minion of Al-Qaeda. The signs are the same and the result is the same.

Despite all of our experience with these incidents of mass murder and attempted murder, we continue to be surprised by attacks on our own soil—the 2012 slaughter of school children in Sandy Hook Elementary and the 2013 Boston Marathon bombings. With each incident, we look back and search for that one sign that we should have seen, or someone should have seen, the sign that we should look for in order to stop this from ever happening again. Law enforcement, the news media, and our political leaders all meet, review, discuss, and debate what to do "next time."

Meanwhile, the Insider Threat continues to plague our society. We have seen it in the military, not only with my own story of Hasan Akbar, but also with Major Nidal Hasan, an Army psychologist, convicted for the November 5, 2009, shooting deaths of 13 soldiers and wounding of 32 more in Fort Hood, TX. We see it also with civilians, as we did in June 2009, when the civilian Abdulhakim Mujahid Muhammad opened fired on Army soldiers at an Army Recruiting Station in Little Rock, AK, killing one person.

We have seen the Insider Threat explode in public places by attackers such as Timothy McVeigh, who was convicted of the April 19, 1995, bombing of the Alfred P. Murrah Building in downtown Oklahoma City which killed 168 people and injured 600; James Holmes, who is accused of killing 12 and wounding 70 in a mass shooting in a movie theater in Aurora, CO; and the Tsarnaev brothers, who are suspected of the 2013 Boston Marathon bombing that brutally killed three and wounded more than 264 others.

Not all of the attacks are successful. For example, in November 2010, a 19-year-old student of Oregon State University was arrested after using his cell phone to try to detonate what he thought were explosives in a van. The bomb was actually a dummy bomb manufactured by FBI agents. The furthest thing from the bomber's mind was law enforcement officials' ability to prevent the attack before it happened. According to an FBI affidavit, the student said, "It's in Oregon, and Oregon, like you know, nobody ever thinks about Oregon."

In reality, destroyers of the American dream are living right next door to us, going to school with our children and befriending them, all while implementing a cunning plan to kill them. How do we combat this in America without weakening the American resolve to treat everyone fairly?

After each incident, we say, "he was a loner," or "he was picked on," or "he seemed like such a sweet man," or "he was a normal kid who did normal stuff." We tend to look at most of these attackers as one monolithic entity—single males aged 17-45. However, the truth is that no single, definitive profile exists.

If it did, the problem would be more easily solved.

We are aware that some people and organizations have pure and genuine hatred for America, its people, and its way of life. However, they are not the only Insider Threat.

What my experience and research has revealed is there is no such thing as "The One Sign." The reason that the Insider Threat succeeds is that the signs are small and develop a pattern of idiosyncrasy that emerges over time. Alone, most signs are not that clear, or they are so small that we dismiss them.

Therefore, we need to stop ignoring our "gut feelings" and begin to respect our instincts.

* * *

Not too long ago, in a typical college classroom, the mostly male students and the professor began discussing weapons and guns, and the subject of who had or owned a gun came up. The discussion was calm and at times even humorous.

One student said that he not only owned a gun, but that it was inside of his car parked in the campus parking lot. Almost the entire class, including the professor, acted as if the comment was funny. All except one 19-year-old student.

He acted on his instincts and reported what had happened in the class to a school administrator, telling him, "I don't know it to be true, but it sounded quite matter-of-fact. You can take it as you please. I just felt that I needed to tell you."

The administrator called in the student who claimed to have a gun and told him, "Let's take a walk," never mentioning where they were going or why. As they started across campus, the administrator notified the student of the institution's policy allowing random searches at their discretion, and then revealed to him what was about to take place. Within a block of the parking lot, the student stopped and said, "Okay, I want you to know that I have an AK-47 assault rifle in the trunk of my car."

In this case, no malicious intent was ever planned. He had planned to connect with a friend to store the gun at his house in the rural area of the state where he lived. The father of the friend had consented to storing the gun for weekend target practice in the woods near their home.

In this case, the signs displayed were taken seriously, and the situation was addressed. Although incidences such as this one where no actual threat exists will occur, we can no longer assume that these signs are meaningless.

I am convinced that there is always a subtle sign, if we just listen and act.

In light of some recent events, a few mentioned here, the U.S. Department of Homeland Security has affirmed that the Insider Threat is not just someone who looks differently, talks differently, or prays differently. In an effort to build awareness, they've instituted a program called See Something, Say Something, which is based on the idea that "an alert public plays a critical role in keeping our nation safe."

Through See Something, Say Something, the Department of Homeland Security asks that the public report suspicious activities to their local law enforcement agencies, rather than staying silent. They realize that we have come to a point where we can no longer rely solely on federal agents to track down every Insider Threat, especially those who are embedded. Our citizens have long been responsible for the apprehension of Insider Threat plots. That vigilance must continue if our country is to remain safe.

In order to avoid civil rights violations, Homeland Security offers the following guidelines:

> "Factors such as race, ethnicity, national origin, or religious affiliation alone are not suspicious. For that reason, the public should report only suspicious behavior and situations (e.g., an unattended backpack in a public place or someone trying to break into a restricted area) rather than beliefs, thoughts, ideas, expressions, associations, or speech unrelated to terrorism or other criminal activity. Only reports that document behavior reasonably indicative of criminal activity related to terrorism will be shared with federal partners."

In addition to this national call for help, I have found the following strategies could help us all to uncover Insider Threats— or even better—to stop them:

1. **Trust No One** – The Insider Threat means that we must even be willing to look at our innermost circle of friends and family for signs that they are feeling disconnected and want to harm a particular person, company, organization, or group of people.

   This is difficult because you may feel a strong sense of loyalty, and therefore as though you are betraying a loved one, when turning someone close to you into the authorities. However, you would be in a perfect position to notice the subtle changes of frustration or paranoia that often occur just before an attack. And you could be the person to help divert the attack by getting that friend or family member the help they need.

2. **Observe – Listen – Report** – We must all be more vigilant now. With the proliferation of social media and the ability to Google how to make homemade bombs, some people who may have never acted on their violent compulsions now have the tools at their fingertips to make a very large and damaging impact—and to do so under the radar of law enforcement. Therefore, it is up to each of us to make sure we report any suspicions of violent or potentially violent behavior.

3. **Know Your Neighbor** – We don't know people like we used to. We are so busy with our smart phones, tablets, laptop computers, and various other technologies that we barely notice what is happening around us.

   Our culture has changed over the years, and it is imperative that we gradually get back to being a bit more personal. We need to take the time to build stronger relationships in the workplace, as well as in our neighborhoods, classrooms, and our local coffee shops.

   Organizational leaders need to take the time to build cohesive teams. The hierarchy of the leadership needs to start showing that they care. If we weave more compassion into all of our interactions, we can begin to help people develop the emotional tools needed to deal with difficult situations that occur. Otherwise, we can inadvertently contribute to building an explosive situation.

4. **Listen, Don't Just Hear** – Listen to those around you and take comments seriously. Far too many times, after someone has committed a crime someone will say, "I knew something sounded, looked, or seemed suspicious."

My point here is to act on your instinct, and report it immediately. Start with your boss, your neighborhood watch leaders, or other local leader. If you feel immediately threatened, do not hesitate to contact 9-1-1. Do not worry who is the "right person." Any community leader should know where to direct you. There is not just one solution.

When you do make your report, be sure you give as much detail as possible. Describe the threat and the person or group involved and everything you know about the incident, such as where and when it happened.

The U.S. Department of Homeland Security makes clear that when reporting, you must remember that a person and his or her clothing, nationality, race, or religion are not considered threats. Only actions or threats of actions are considered threats.

5. **Gut Check** – If a family member, friend, coworker, or acquaintance says something that sounds odd to you—anything from alluding to troubles at home or violent physical or verbal abuse at work—ask questions, even if you feel worried that they will take your questions "the wrong way." It is okay to be embarrassed—your embarrassment may save someone's life. No one ever really died from embarrassment.

Opening yourself up and asking the personal questions after hearing something that does not pass your "gut check" will help bring small problems to light before they get too big. You can find ways to show that you are being compassionate and not nosy. Offer to assist them in finding help, or to continue to talk about their frustrations.

If you continue to feel that the person is escalating in their threatening behavior, then report them to your Human Resources department, on-site security, or local police. They are better equipped to identify real threats and have the tools to deal with them.

While these are all key tips on how to sniff out the next Insider Threat, we must each strike our own balance between being vigilant and being paranoid. No amount of vigilance will catch all Insider Threats. The point to take away is that we can no longer rely solely on federal agents to track down every terrorist, especially those embedded in our country.

However daunting to consider, the Boston marathon bombing will not be the last of its kind. There will continue to be groups and individuals looking for opportunities of similar devastation. More daunting is the fact that anyone could be the terrorist and carry out the terrorist attack.

Despite these sobering facts of life, it is possible to incorporate this new way of thinking into your daily routine and still enjoy and live your life to the fullest, embracing all that your community has to offer. Do not let the fear of terrorism stop you, but instead, pay attention and listen to your instincts so that it does not have that chance.

The Insider Threat is very real—there is no definitive profile—and it's closer than you think.

# # #

ABOUT THE AUTHOR

(Ret.) Command Sergeant Major Bart E. Womack is the recipient of two Bronze Stars, one for Valor. Serving in positions of great responsibility throughout the period of 18 February 1977 through 30 June 2006, his career is distinguished by exceptional meritorious service. His evaluations list him as the standard by which others are measured. (Ret.) CSM Bart Womack distinguished himself as a consummate trainer of soldiers by consistently demonstrating the highest standards of military discipline, professionalism, and leadership.

Attaining one of the highest honors in the Army, he served at The Tomb of the Unknown Soldier as a Sentinel and Relief Commander. Later he served as the Sergeant of the Guard, interfacing with the President of the United States, the Honorable George Bush, and the Honorable Bill Clinton, as well as former Soviet Leader Mikhail Gorbachev and other leaders on the world stage at numerous nationally televised wreath ceremonies.

During Operation Iraqi Freedom and throughout the Global War on Terror, CSM Womack made significant contributions to the Army and the NCO Corps by providing focus, leadership, and mentorship to all officers and enlisted soldiers who had the privilege to serve with him, regardless of location, situation, or enemy action.

By virtue of his experience and knowledge of contemporary operations of the 101st Airborne Division (Air Assault) and Fort Campbell, CSM Womack was selected to serve as the interim Division Command Sergeant Major from January through March 2005. Like his exemplary performances before, CSM Womack was able to execute the duties of that office while simultaneously balancing the duties of the Commandant of the NCO Academy.

This exceptional noncommissioned officer has served the United States Army with distinction for nearly three decades as a professional soldier. He is not only a tactical and technical expert but also displays dedication and discipline associated with only the finest America has to offer. His maturity, expertise, and personal dedication to excellence have contributed immeasurably to the readiness of the United States Army and the security of our Great Nation.

Since retiring, CSM Womack has worked in the entertainment industry, as an actor and a Military Technical Advisor for feature films and television. Recently he spent 18 months in Afghanistan, training the Afghanistan National Army and its senior enlisted leadership at the Corps level. He has spent time in Nigeria, as part of the Africa Contingency Operation, training that country's Army. He volunteers his free time by mentoring Army ROTC Cadets. Additionally, he works with returning Veterans in the Saddles for Soldiers program, which through the use of horses, is designed to help veterans and their families better cope with the trauma and stressors that often come with returning from combat; long term depression, reestablishment of life skills, and readjustment into civilian life. He proudly adds the title of 'Author' to his resume.

Connect with Bart on LinkedIn –
http://www.linkedin.com/pub/bart-womack/17/704/281

Join the Conversation with Bart on Facebook –
https://www.facebook.com/bartwomackauthor

Join the Conversation with Bart on Twitter –
https://twitter.com/BartWomack

Visit the Website for More Information –
http://embeddedenemy.com/index.html